The

PRAYERS & PERSONAL
DEVOTIONS
of
MOTHER
ANGELICA

ALSO BY RAYMOND ARROYO

Mother Angelica

*Mother Angelica's Little Book of
Life Lessons and Everyday Spirituality*

*Mother Angelica's Private and
Pithy Lessons from the Scriptures*

The
PRAYERS & PERSONAL
DEVOTIONS
of
MOTHER
ANGELICA

INTRODUCED AND EDITED BY
RAYMOND ARROYO

DOUBLEDAY
New York London Toronto Sydney Auckland

CID
DOUBLEDAY

Published in the United States by Doubleday Religion,
an imprint of the Crown Publishing Group,
a division of Random House, Inc., New York.
www.crownpublishing.com

DOUBLEDAY and the DD colophon are
registered trademarks of Random House, Inc.

Library of Congress Cataloging-in-Publication Data
M. Angelica (Mary Angelica), Mother, 1923–
The prayers and personal devotions of Mother Angelica /
introduced and edited by Raymond Arroyo. — 1st ed.
p. cm.
1. M. Angelica (Mary Angelica), Mother, 1923–   2. Prayers.
I. Arroyo, Raymond.   II. Title.
BX4705.M124A25 2010
242'.802 — dc22   2009045512

ISBN 978-0-307-58825-8

Printed in the United States of America

Design by Leonard W. Henderson

2   4   6   8   10   9   7   5   3   1

First Edition

For Raymond and Lynda Arroyo

Who taught me how to pray

CONTENTS

Contents

INTRODUCTION

Given her trademark outspokenness and ubiquitous presence in the media for nearly thirty years, it is easy to overlook the hidden foundation of Mother Angelica's life: prayer.

Prayer is one of those intensely personal acts that few execute well and even fewer practice with regularity. For Mother Angelica it was "a way of life." She prayed as creatively as anyone I have ever encountered and approached the practice from a diversity of angles. Mother could be lost in contemplation, speaking intimately to God as "a friend" one moment and in the next, leading her nuns in a time-tested litany. Beyond the required prayers of her religious community, this Poor Clare of Perpetual Adoration used assorted modes of prayer to reach God and to remain in His presence throughout the day. Her definition of prayer was simple: "to empty ourselves and to be filled with the Trinity."

A sister who lived with Mother Angelica for more than a quarter of a century offered this insight: "Mother prayed constantly. She was very busy, but you always felt like she was at prayer with God. She had the gift of gab around people, but in the car, or whenever she had to travel, she was quiet—totally silent. Very contemplative. She was always at prayer. Even now in her bed, many times you ask her a question and she won't answer because she is so wrapped up in God."

For Mother Angelica prayer was a habit developed early in her religious life and nurtured over almost seven decades. The dazzling fruit of her temporal existence was rooted in her prayer life. This was the source of so many of her inspirations and a well of solace in her darkest hours. Mother's approach to prayer (like so many things in her life) was innovative and practical. Her goal was to pray without ceasing at every moment of the day, no matter where she found herself.

"Everything you do is for God—though your attention, your activity is focused on the duties of life," Mother Angelica instructed her sisters. "This way there is no separation between your life and your prayer; they are woven together like threads in a tapestry. . . . It is very simple to pray without ceasing. It means living in the Present Moment. That's all it takes, and you can do that wherever you are. Sometimes that union with God and that unceasing prayer is a prayer of anguish, a prayer of tears, or a prayer of joy."

This work is a repository of her favorite prayers, both improvised as well as time-tested compositions. They are filled with anguish and joy, touching on all aspects of life and its varied stages.

The book you are holding completes a cycle of Mother Angelica works that I initiated in 1999. In my biography *Mother Angelica: The Remarkable Story of a Nun, Her Nerve, and a Network of Miracles*, I laid bare the facts of Mother's incredible story in a dramatic narrative. With *Mother Angelica's Little Book of Life Lessons and Everyday Spirituality* and the ensuing *Mother Angelica's Private and Pithy Lessons from the Scriptures,* I collaborated with Mother and her nuns to give the public access to her spiritual advice and inspired Scriptural teachings.

This book is the most active of the canon. It is a collection meant to be experienced and used, prayed and contemplated. In some ways it is a spiritual biography told through the diverse prayers either recited or composed by Mother Angelica over her long life. The book is also an intimate glimpse of Mother's soul; for these are the prayers, devotions, and meditations that fired her spirit and united her will to God's own.

The sixteenth-century essayist Michel de Montaigne once said: "There are few men who dare to publish to the world the prayers they make to Almighty God." Mother Angelica dares that and more in this remarkable collection.

On the pages that follow you will find the prayers Mother recited as a young novice and professed nun; the private prayers she composed as an abbess in her Birmingham chapel; a never before published diary written during a prolonged "Dark Night of the Soul" experience; private meditations she offered to her sisters; some of her very earliest teachings; and the personal devotions she regularly prayed and later propagated.

Resuming my collaboration with Our Lady of the Angels Monastery and Mother Angelica, I was granted access to materials that have been hidden away in their monastery archives for decades. Much of what follows has never been published before. Some of these prayers were composed by Mother on yellow legal pads in her own hand. Others were discovered on bits of paper, addressed to particular nuns. Selected devotions are drawn in the Poor Clares of Perpetual Adoration Prayer Book that Mother began using when she first entered the cloister. These are rare and precious supplications and praises. Now they can live on.

Taken as a whole, the contents provide insight into the marvelous flexibility of Mother Angelica's prayer life and the ease of communication she enjoyed with her Spouse. As one of her sisters told me: "She would go into the chapel and talk to Jesus as if He were an Italian." That passionate, conversational approach runs throughout these pages as well.

"Prayer is not something, it is Someone," Mother often said, "and that Someone is Jesus." May her words and these cherished devotions draw you closer to God and cause you to respond to His promptings as Mother Angelica would.

Raymond Arroyo
August 15, 2009
Feast of the Assumption
Northern Virginia

The

PRAYERS & PERSONAL
DEVOTIONS

of

MOTHER
ANGELICA

O God, Holy Ghost,

Who didst inspire the author of this book with Thy
light, and art, thus teaching us and permitting us to
hear Thy voice and also Thy divine instructions,
grant us the grace to understand them rightly, that
relishing them and practicing them in all our actions,
for Thy greater honor and for our progress in
perfection, we may know Thee, O God,
more perfectly and love Thee more ardently.

O Blessed Virgin Mary, implore for us this grace.
Amen.

—*Poor Clares of Perpetual Adoration Prayer Book*

I stand before You, Lord God, a sinner. In all the
realms of Your creation no one is more undeserving of
Your love than I. This is why I dare approach Your
Presence. Your power is at its best in weakness,
Your love is more gratuitous to the ungrateful, and
Your mercy more sublime to the undeserving.

—*Mother Angelica*

The

PRIVATE PRAYERS

At The Start of Day

PRAYER IN THE MORNING

Good morning, Jesus. I want to give You this day with all my love. I want to unite my every thought and action with every thought and action of Your earthly life. Help me to be kind and patient. It looks like a difficult day—a day of decision and I'm not sure of the right course to take. A day of pain and I feel weak, a day of uncertainty and I tend to lose hope. Don't let me forget Your Abiding Love and Providence today. Walk beside me and when I hesitate put Your arms around me and steady my faltering steps. Guide me in Your paths and give me that assurance that comes with Faith; Faith in Your Promises, Faith in Your Love.

PRAYER BEFORE WORK

In Nomine Patris, et Filii, et Spiritus Sancti. Amen.

To Thy love, O my God, I consecrate all the work and actions of this day, in union with those of Thy beloved Son whilst here on earth, and with His purest intentions. I offer them through the Immaculate Heart of Mary to Thy greater glory and in the spirit of adoration of the Most Blessed Sacrament. Hail Mary . . . (PCPA Prayer Book)

AN OFFERING OF WORK

My Father, accept the work of my hands today in union with the labor of Jesus during His life. I offer to You the fatigue and tension of this day in union with the weariness of Jesus as He walked from town to town. My actions are imperfect, my motives are often selfish, but everything I do this day I unite with the most pure motives of Jesus and His perfect life. I desire to please You alone and to love You with the love of the Holy Spirit.

PRAYER AT WORK

Lord God, show me Your Will in my life. Give me the work that is best suited to the talents You have given me. Bless me with fellow workers who will help me stay close to You. Grant that my work may not be a source of disturbance or temptation. Give me the strength to do it well and enthusiastically and bless my efforts to witness to Your love. Give me a just wage and do not permit me to desire more than I deserve. Bless my employer and give him the wisdom to use the gifts You have given him for Your honor and glory. Lord Jesus, do not permit me to lose sight of Your Presence in my soul today. Quiet the noise around me so I may hear the soft whisper of Your Voice.

Humility and Pardon

A PRAYER FOR HUMILITY

You've got to watch your own thoughts. When you are conscious of an unloving, unkind, critical, or hateful thought against anyone; whether present or elsewhere, check it immediately. Strike your breast and say:

"Jesus, if it wasn't for you, I wouldn't be able to breathe. Be merciful to me, a poor sinner."

Humble yourself, and you'll be surprised how good that other person looks. It's because we're not humble that we have the effrontery to tear other people down.

TO BE HUMBLE OF HEART

In the world, my Lord, one must be great to speak to the great but with You one must be small and of little account. It is only when I think of Your greatness and majesty that I realize how pride must offend You. How can a small, created being rear its head in defiance of Omnipotence? It is truly a manifestation of Your Mercy and Love that You do not annihilate me when I defy Your Law and reject Your Love. O Humble God, make me humble of heart.

Few souls understand what God would accomplish in them if they were to abandon themselves unreservedly to Him and if they were to allow His grace to mold them accordingly.

—*St. Ignatius Loyola*

PRAYER FOR PARDON

Lord God, I ask pardon for all our sins: For all the times we've offended You in thought, word, or deed; for the selfishness in our lives and the ego that blocks You out of our minds and hearts. I ask pardon for the distractions that keep leading us away from You. I ask Your mercy upon us, and on the whole world. Prepare our hearts and minds, Lord, for what is to come. Prepare our souls, our thoughts, our will, and give us strength to fight the good fight. Give us communal love, Lord, the kind that will bind us together as one in the heart of Jesus. We ask Lord, small and insignificant as we are, that we may give you comfort and love. We ask for pardon, Lord, for those who crowned you with thorns by their pride and arrogance. We ask pardon for those who scourge you at the pillar by their immorality. Lord, we ask pardon for those who strip You of Your garments by their greed and ambition for worldly things. We ask pardon for all priests and religious who have been nailed to the cross with vows and have not been faithful. We ask pardon for all mankind, for the whole world, for all of our sins. Be merciful to us, Lord. We praise and glorify Your name, for You are holy, You alone. Glorify Your justice, Lord and Your mercy. We praise and bless You. Amen.

PRAYER FOR KINDNESS

Dear Jesus, make me kind. I look at Your life and Your kindness stands out like a lone star on a dark night. No matter how tired You were You always had time for the sick, poor sinners, children, and all those in need. Your Heart had sympathy for their weaknesses and You reached out to them with loving compassion. When I feel impatient with the frailties of my neighbor, Lord Jesus, grant that I may not only think of Your kindness but stop for a moment and enter into it; let me *feel* Your kindness in the depths of my soul so that my prayer will not be empty. I need to participate in Your kindness if I am to be kind. I cannot do it on my own. My poor soul tends to be critical of others and this makes me impatient and unkind. You understood human nature so well that You gave everyone an opportunity to repent. You never picked out the trivial faults of Your Apostles or demanded exterior perfection. The only time You corrected them was when the faults they committed were deeply interior and endangered their union with You and the Father. Jealousy, ambition, and greed were the faults that You quickly brought out into the open so You could cleanse the Apostles of these dangerous temptations. Give me the grace, Lord Jesus, to distinguish between faults of character that form part of my neighbor's temperament and evil tendencies that destroy grace in his soul. Help me to endure the former with love and to correct the latter with courage. Help me to love the sinner but never condone his sin. Please, dear Jesus, let me first remove the beam from my own eye before I even see the splinter in the eye of my neighbor.

GRATITUDE AND SELF-KNOWLEDGE

Lord Jesus, I feel so sad every time I think of the nine lepers who never returned to say "Thank You." It is hard to conceive of anyone so selfish, and yet how often do I remember to thank You for all the gifts and graces You have given to me? It is so easy to see faults in other people and completely overlook my own. Are the faults I see in others a mirror of my own soul? Gentle Jesus, I recoil at the prospect that what I see in others must be in me. If this is true, and I fear it is, would not this be a step toward self-knowledge?

TO FORGIVE AND FORGET

Lord, I need Your help—help to love those who do not love me in return. I find this so difficult. What must You feel when You love *me* and I turn away! I need Your grace to forgive and forget. Injustice cries out for revenge and old memories bring back old wounds that smart and sting. Cover my poor soul with the healing balm of love and compassion. Make me unselfish sweet Jesus, so I will be content with just loving and count it a privilege to forgive even seventy times seven.

Practical Pleas

PRAYER TO OBTAIN FAVORS

This prayer comes from the Poor Clares of Perpetual Adoration Prayer Book that Mother used as a young sister. It is believed that those who recite this prayer fifteen times daily from the feast of St. Andrew (November 30) until Christmas will receive what they ask.

Hail! and blessed be the hour and moment in which the Son of God was born of the most pure Virgin in Bethlehem, at midnight, in piercing cold. In that hour vouchsafe, O my God, to hear my prayers and grant my desires, through the merits of our Savior Jesus Christ and of His Virgin Mother. Amen.

A PRAYER OF SUPPLICATION

Knowing Your Infinite Goodness, I dare to ask for all the material and spiritual things I need to live on this earth and to safely arrive in the Kingdom. I ask for work and the strength to accomplish it well. I ask for health when that condition is necessary for my well-being. I ask for pain when it will prune my soul or prevent me from walking the path of sin. I ask for good friends—friends that love me for myself and will stay by me in success and failure. I ask for peace in my family—the kind of peace that is built on love and forbearance. I ask for the forgiveness of my sins and the sins of the whole world. I ask for virtue, especially that particular virtue that will help me overcome my predominant fault—the fault that is the cause of most of my failures. I ask that You bless my enemies, especially those who have offended me out of jealousy or hatred. Do not permit them to live or die in that state of misery but give them the grace to see the light and turn to You in true repentance. Console those whom I have offended, hurt, or displeased, Lord Jesus. I am sorry for all those weaknesses in me that are a stumbling block to my neighbor. Do not permit him to waver or lose faith on my account. I ask for all the things I think I need and for all the things You know I need.

> The reason why sometimes you have asked and not received, is because you have asked amiss, either inconsistently, or lightly, or because you have asked for what was not good for you, or because you have ceased asking.
>
> —*St. Basil*

A PRAYER DURING FINANCIAL HARDSHIP

Praise and bless You in Your Holy Name. Lord, we ask that you bestow upon us the funds so that we may continue to know and love and serve You. You know Your Enemy is after us and after Your work—so that it might fail. Lord, we ask that You help us, that You will give us the peace and joy that comes from total trust in Your loving providence. We place this in Your hands. You know what we need. You know what it costs to sustain us every day, every week, every month. Bless us with Your bountiful generosity. We ask this in the name of the Father and in Jesus' name. Amen.

PRAYER DURING A MOMENT OF TRANSITION

Mother composed this prayer in the year 2000 for sisters about to take their solemn vows and progress in their religious life. But it applies to anyone who finds themselves in transition.

Lord Jesus, it has been a long time arriving at this special day. Years have passed, crosses have been borne, doubts have been conquered, temptations fought. The years that at times seem so long, have at last come to fruition. Your Providence led the way, Your Compassion made the path, Your Mercy carried me through and at last, I have arrived, at this day of all days.

Bring to my mind, Sweet Lord of my Heart, all that I have learned, fought for, and conquered, so that the rest of my life I may ever remember Your Love and carry out Your Will, lovingly and cheerfully, to the end of my days.

Thank You for Your Grace and let me ever be Your faithful disciple. Amen.

A PRAYER TO RECOGNIZE GOD IN THE WORLD

Give me the grace, dear Jesus, to see You in my neighbor, to see Your Purity in the smile of a child, Your Power in the accomplishments of men, Your Providence in daily events, Your Wisdom in the aged, and Your Goodness in my neighbor. Let youth portray Your Joy and the whole world witness to Your Love. Grant, sweet Jesus, that I, too, may manifest You to the world.

FOR THE COUNTRY AND ITS LEADERS

Lord God, bless my Country and all those who lead its people. The temptations of those who hold office are great and the Enemy uses the glory of this world to choke Your Word from their minds. Look upon this great Country with mercy and compassion. Grant that only those men who are capable of authority may possess that power. Give the people of this land the light and grace to seek first the Kingdom and put their trust in You rather than the things of this world. Take away from us all greed and worldly ambitions and make us a people full of love, mercy, and compassion. Let this Nation always live under Your Law and guidance and under the principles Your Son gave us. In You, Lord God, we put our trust.

A PRAYER FOR FAMILIES

Lord Father, bless our families. Make each family in this great Nation a beautiful image of the Trinity. Inspire husbands and fathers to imitate Your Compassion and Mercy. Let them be humble servants who seek only Your Glory and the good of their loved ones. Let them be good guides, protectors, providers, and, most of all, builders of holy lives. As Head of the Family give them loving hearts that they may never be domineering over those You have placed under their care.

Inspire wives and mothers, Lord Father, with a deep realization of their role as the heart of their family. Give them the fortitude to be an example of self-sacrifice and a means of reconciliation. Let them portray the gentleness of Jesus and the love of the Holy Spirit. Give them the Gift of Counsel so they may have that special intuition to discern Your Will in their family situation. Let them be a source of strength to their husbands and a source of understanding to their children.

Inspire the children of our families to be obedient members of a love-filled household. Let them be thoughtful and loving to parents and humbly learn from the experience and wisdom of the old. Grant, dear Lord, that the families of this Nation may be bound together by a self-sacrificing love and may grow in Your Grace by united prayer. Give them the light to face their problems with courage and let them manifest the image of Your Trinity in their lives.

PRAYER BEFORE TRAVEL

Lord Jesus, protect me as I travel today. Give me the alertness to see danger and the wisdom to avoid it. Let me be cautious and patient with fellow-travelers. Let me radiate You to all I meet and let the car, train, or plane be filled with Your Presence so I may carry You wherever I go.

PRAYER FOR THE WAYWARD

O God, those I love have turned away from You. They go down a dangerous path and my words are without power. I am helpless to give them light, but You, oh God, desire all men to be saved and in Your hands is the power to touch the most hardened hearts. Bring them back to the right path and give them the grace to love You with their whole hearts and to desire nothing but You. Tell me, my Lord, what can I say to them? How can I reach them?

Say to them: "Take courage, my children, call on God: He will deliver you from tyranny, from the hands of your enemies; for I look to the Eternal for your rescue, and joy has come to me from the Holy One. In sorrow and tears I watched you go away, but God will give you back to me in joy and gladness forever."

My children, patiently bear the anger brought on you by God. Your enemy has persecuted you, but soon you will witness his destruction and set your foot on his neck.
—Baruch 4:21–23, 25

A PRAYER FOR ENEMIES

Lord, bless my enemies. Give them the grace to see the light, and if I am the cause of their hatred, give me the light to see my weaknesses. I wish them the blessings of this life and the next. Let my forgiveness merit for them more grace, and grant that I may forgive with all my heart. Let us all meet one day in Your Kingdom where all those personality weaknesses will be gone and we shall see each other in You alone.

FOR TRUST IN OLD AGE

Every day, my Jesus, I feel and see myself getting older. Sometimes it frightens me and at other times I rejoice. I am frightened because I fear the pain and disappointments of old age. I rejoice because I am closer to the Kingdom and to that beautiful day when we will see each other face-to-face. I need trust, dear Lord, to put every moment of my life in Your hands. I need that confidence that looks to the Spirit within me—the Spirit that is and will be forever young and full of joy. Teach me, my Jesus, that You have kept the best wine till now and that the latter years of my life can be the most powerful because I have more time for You, more time to pray, more time to think of Your Attributes and Your Kingdom. Dispel my doubts, increase my faith, and grant that the Hope You have instilled into my soul may blossom out into trust and confidence in Your promises.

> Listen to me. . . . You who have been carried since birth, whom I have carried since the time you were born. In your old age I shall still be the same. When your hair is gray I shall still support you. I have already done so. I have carried you; I shall still support and deliver you.
>
> *—Isaiah 46:3, 4*

Follow your own way of speaking to our Lord sincerely, lovingly, confidently, and simply, as your heart dictates.

—*St. Jane Frances de Chantal*

PRAYER WHEN WAITING

Lord Jesus, make me patient. I get so irritated when waiting is demanded of me. I wait for appointments, doctors, clerks, and red lights. I wait for my neighbors to express themselves and change bad habits. I wait for morning to come and when it comes I find myself waiting for night. I wait for my own faults and weaknesses to be overcome and for sickness to pass. I wait for each season to come and go and I reluctantly wait as old age overtakes me. It seems, dear Lord, that I spend half my life waiting for something or someone, and mostly I wait in an ill-mannered and ill-tempered way. Give me the patience that was such a beautiful part of Your life on earth, the kind that waits with love and serenity. I need patience that uses every spare moment to speak to You, love You, and meditate upon Your attributes. Let me look upon these moments as precious jewels presented to me by Your Hand. Let me use this valuable time to say all the prayers I never have time for, to recall Your words in Scripture, to see Your face in creation and to recognize Your plan in my life. Let me see "waiting" as extra time allotted to me to worship and love You. Let me be peacefully and lovingly patient so I may radiate Your Compassion.

PRAYER FOR THE GOOD USE OF TIME

Thank You, Holy Trinity, for Your Goodness to me. You care for me as if I were alone in the world. Give me the grace to see Your Providence and solicitude in every detail of my life. As I look forward to "tomorrow" never let me forget it is always "today." I have already begun the eternal "now" that shall never have an end. Holy Father, let me see time as a precious commodity that must be used well and never wasted. Give me the right perspective on time so I will realize how quickly it passes. Give me the discernment to invest it wisely so it will reap rich dividends for Eternity. Do not permit it to run through my fingers like sand falling to the ground, without purpose or strength. Increase my gift of time that I may reap a hundredfold. God of Power, who drew me out of nothingness, mold me into a perfect image of You so the world may see Your Holiness.

Prayers in Difficulty

PRAYER FOR ACCEPTANCE OF SUFFERING

Jesus, I accept whatever suffering I will have for myself, for those I love, and for those who love me. I give this all to you Lord as just and right and holy, only let me love Thee. Amen.

WHEN COLDNESS SETS IN

Lord Jesus, the day is cold and my soul feels the chill of luke-warmness. The fervor of yesterday is gone and the darkness of tomorrow already casts its shadow upon me. Hide me in Your warm Heart, sweet Jesus, and let the fire of that Infinite Love consume the dross covering my soul like a fine dust. Let my imperfections be changed into virtues, my weakness into strength, my doubts into Faith, and my discouragement into Hope. Take my Will, Lord Jesus, and unite it in such a close union with Your Will that it is One with You. The chill is gone, dear Lord. Talking to You has warmed my cold heart.

A PRAYER IN WEAKNESS

O God, my eyes fill with tears when I think of my sins and in-gratitude. Shall I ever be what You want me to be, or is the striving for holiness a matter of rising and falling? My weak-nesses obsess me at times and Your Mercy is absent from my mind. Thoughts of despair fill my soul and I seem convinced that so holy a God would not love a weak creature like myself. Give me the realization of Your Love—the love that finds its joy in weakness.

I have chosen you, not rejected you. Do not be afraid for I am with you; stop being anxious and watch-ful, for I am your God. I give you strength, I bring you help. I uphold you with My victorious right hand.

Yes, all those who raged against you shall be put to shame and confusion; they who fought against you shall be destroyed and perish.

—Isaiah 41:9

A PRAYER FOR PATIENCE

Every day, my Jesus, I learn by some situation or experience of my great need of You. When I try to be patient on my own, my patience is forced and short-lived. It is obvious to everyone that I am desperately trying to be patient. When I raise my mind and heart to You, dear Jesus, and see You so serenely patient, my soul drinks in that spirit of patience, like a cool breeze on a humid night. Your Patience penetrates my being and only then am I truly patient. It takes so long to learn that I can bear fruit only in You.

PRAYER IN CONFUSION

My Lord, how shall I know Your Will and how shall I discern between good and evil? There are so many dilemmas in my life—dilemmas that are difficult to solve—weaknesses that seem impossible to overcome. Where shall I turn? To whom shall I go?

I will instruct you and teach you the way to go; I will watch over you and be your adviser.

—Psalms 32:8

> **Do what you can and pray for what you cannot yet do.**
> —*St. Augustine*

A PRAYER DURING DOUBT

I have been sorely tempted today, dear Jesus—tempted to doubt that all the things that happen to me are in some way for my good. Sometimes everything seems so wrong and everyone unfair. It is as if I were alone and no one understood. I look to You, and You, too, seem not to care. But in the midst of this darkness and confusion there is always a tiny light to give me courage. There is down deep in my soul a Voice that seems to say, "Fear not—I am with you." I put myself in Your Providence and Mercy for I realize, as never before, that in the darkness Your arms are ever around me.

PRAYER DURING DURESS

My Lord, there is violence everywhere. The darkness brings fear to souls because of the evil intentions in the hearts of men. The enemy lurks in hiding waiting to take advantage of every small weakness in our human nature. The world, dear Lord, offers false ideals and greed is rampant wherever I go. It seems we have strayed far from Your designs for us and we are in great need of your saving help.

They will fight against you but will not overcome you, because I am with you to save you and deliver you—it is Yahweh who speaks. I mean to deliver you from the hands of the wicked and redeem you from the clutches of the violent.

—Jeremiah 15:20–21

FOR PEACE IN CHAOS

My Lord, the world is in a state of chaos. There are shortages, poverty, injustice, and violence. I know it is so because we have strayed from Your Love. We have become puffed up with our own importance and we attribute every good thing to ourselves. We run after the things of this world and forget Your Kingdom. It is a frightening experience Lord Father, to find ourselves in a position where pride prevents us from running to You, and selfishness moves us to more self-seeking. Shall we succumb to evil or will you look upon us with pity and lift us out of this lukewarmness by Your Infinite Mercy?

Take courage, my children, call on God: He who brought disaster on you will remember you as by your will you first strayed away from God, so now turn back and search for him ten times as hard, for as he brought down those disasters on you, so will He rescue you and give you eternal joy.

—Baruch 4: 27–29

A PRAYER IN TRIAL

My Lord and Father, I find there are so many limits to my love. I love You under some circumstances but then forget You under others. It is so easy to proclaim my love for You when all goes well and I feel Your arms around me, but let the cold wind of aridity bring on the darkness of discouragement and I rebel against the Cross. I speak eloquently of Your pruning power but I fear the days when the light of Your Holiness exposes my weakness and I see myself as I really am. Grant me the grace to love You in the present moment no matter what it brings to me. Let me see Your pruning and merciful love reshaping my soul into the image of Jesus.

> **My son, when the Lord corrects you, do not treat it lightly, but do not get discouraged when He reprimands you. For the Lord trains the ones that He loves . . . suffering is part of your training. God is treating you as His sons.**
>
> *—Hebrews 12:5–7*

WHEN YOU CAN'T PRAY

When I have difficulty praying, I just say: "Lord, I offer you all the beautiful prayers that Mary said to You throughout her life, and Catherine of Siena and Angela of Foligno and St. Faustina and Mother Cabrini and all our saints." I mean some of them were very expressive and emotional and poetic. So if you feel you can't pray, offer Him the prayers of those who obviously could.

PRAYER WHEN DISCOURAGED

O God, my mind whirls around in confusion and my soul seems destitute of all consolation. It is as if all the world and all my life were telescoped into one moment and I carry the burden of it all. I cannot see any future except tomorrow being another today. All my yesterdays crowd around me, some accusing and some regret filled. It is like a prison with a thousand voices shouting for attention. Divine Jailor, You have the key to release my soul from the prison of discouragement. Unlock the doors and let me roam freely into the regions of Your Love. Deliver me from the tyranny of my own will. Surely You take no pleasure in my soul disquieted within me, for then I am wrapped in myself. Do I hear You whisper, "Unlock the door for the key is within. I wait ready to enter and comfort you"?

FOR AN INCREASE OF FAITH

Lord Jesus, increase my faith. I want so much to have the kind of faith that moves mountains. I want to believe with such intensity that only a thin veil separates me from seeing You face-to-face. I want to see the Father's Will and providence in everything that happens. You had such a serene confidence in the Father's guiding hand as it manifested His Will in the circumstances of life. Give me that gift, Lord and Master, that I too may have the joy of beholding the Divine Presence in everything that happens to me.

PRAYER DURING UPHEAVAL

My Jesus, my soul is troubled and no matter where I look I find turmoil and a sense of hopelessness. Tension is everywhere in the world, and nations seek to destroy each other by wars. How can I live in this kind of atmosphere and remain untouched by it? How can I pray when there are so many urgent things to do?

> **Peace I bequeath to you, My own peace I give you—
> a peace the world cannot give; this is My gift to you.
> Do not let your heart be troubled or afraid.**
>
> *—John 14:27*

NO FEAR

> **I give thanks to you Yahweh, You were angry with me
> but Your anger is appeased and You have given me
> consolation.**
>
> *—Isaiah 12:1*

Your mercy, oh Lord, astounds me. When I fall it is You who raises me up and pours upon my wounds the balm of Your merciful love. You take the first step at reconciliation and then You open your arms to me as if I were the most faithful of your creatures. Yes, Lord, "I have trust now and have no fear for 'Yahweh is my strength, my song' " (Isaiah 12:2–3).

A PRAYER FOR STRENGTH

Love is a sublime prison. It holds me fast so I do not go headlong to destruction. Your Spirit within me forms an invisible wall that protects me from the spirit of the world, the spirit of lukewarmness, and the spirit of discouragement. I can stand tall, not because of any power of my own but because Your Power is my shield, my weapon, my protection, and my victory.

> A little lifting of the heart suffices; a little remembrance of God, one act of inward worship are prayers which, however short, are nevertheless acceptable to God.
>
> —*Brother Lawrence*

Seeking and Adoring God

PRAYER TO FIND GOD

I do not ask for the riches that perish or the fame that fades away like a morning mist. I only beg for the freedom of a child of God with one goal, one love, one desire: to please You. My heart longs for You, O God. My soul cries out to You. Living without You is like living in a desert devoid of life and beauty. Can it be that the dry sand and scorching heat must sear my soul and cleanse it of all those frailties that make me so unlike You? Must I roam through life seeking and finding You only to lose You again?

PRAYER FOR THE INFINITE

Holy God, though I do not always understand Your Work in my life I trust Your Providence and have Faith in Your Plan. You never take Your eyes from me and yet my eyes wander through the world looking for a place to rest. Why can't I love You as You love me? Why do I seek what is finite when I can possess the Infinite? My fickleness must astound the Angels who see how passing are the things I cling to.

PRAISE OF GOD

Yahweh, there is no one like you. So great are you, so great your mighty name. Who would not revere you, King of Nations? Yes, this is Your due. Since of all the wise among the nations, and in all their kingdoms, there is not a single one like you.

—Jerimiah 10:6–7

My Lord, I often wish I had the words of the great Prophets to tell you of my love and how great I think you are. Accept from my poor heart all the love that is there, and let my mind convey in wordless conversations that You are great and holy.

PRAYER TO INCREASE GOD'S PRESENCE

Lord Trinity, I want to be more aware of Your Divine Presence in my soul. I know Your life with me is often lonely. I flit from one unimportant thing to another and then when my heart becomes empty and lonely I seek You. Why do I run to You only after all else fails? You are the only Light that guides my path, the only Love that is faithful, the only Strength in time of weakness. Be patient with me, Lord, and grant that someday my mind will have no thought that is not pleasing to You and my heart possess no love stronger than its love for You.

TO LIVE IN GOD'S WORLD

Jesus, though crowds surround me, my soul is alone and the silence frightens me. To hear noise outside and feel silence inside gives me the feeling of living in two worlds at the same time. One world clamors for my attention and another for my love. O God, I choose Your World—I choose to roam the limitless realms of Your Love, always seeing new beauty, always hearing the music of Your Merciful Forgiveness.

PRAYER TO HEAR GOD'S VOICE

Why do I constantly resist Your attempts to raise me above myself? Why do I pretend I do not hear the whispers of Your Voice encouraging me to great things while I rest content in petty things? Alas, my Lord, truth forces me to admit that I love myself more than You!

A PRAYER IN NATURE

Holy Spirit, today I want to listen to Your Voice in the beauty of the Father's creation and in the realization of His Love for me. The whole world seems to stand still when I think of His awesome Presence. All the important things in my life fade away and I stand before Him small and insignificant. He listens to my voice as though I were an only child and cares for me with total attention.

IN PRAISE OF THE FATHER AND THE SON

O God, I am humbled by the thought of Your Grandeur! Your Power overwhelms me and Your Infinite Attributes cause my heart to burst forth in songs of praise. Who am I that You should think of me and love me? All I possess comes from Your Goodness. The only things I can call my own are my sins—these are mine. I see You as all Goodness and myself as all weakness. What shall I do when that great gulf between us seems to keep You from me? I know what I shall do, Lord Father. I shall run to Jesus because He has taken upon Himself my weaknesses and He possesses Your Infinite Attributes. He is my bridge, my link, my path, my direction, my shield. When I put my hand in His, I walk the distance between us, Lord Father, with ease and peace. His Precious Blood purifies my weaknesses and His Love makes me like You. He fights my battles with the Enemy and covers my lukewarmness with His Love. Thank You, Father, for giving me Jesus so my journey to You may be lightened and I strengthened by His Spirit.

PRAYER FOR THE DIVINE PRESENCE

Lord Jesus, never let me lose sight of Your Divine Presence in my soul—that mysterious silent Presence that waits so patiently for my love. Your Presence envelops my soul and yet my lukewarmness ignores Your Presence so often that I tend to forget It completely. Is not every moment I spend on superfluities comparable to throwing diamonds in the mud? My soul hungers for You, Lord Jesus, and yet You are present within me. Why do I insist on seeking You outside myself? Is it because when I find You in creation I do not change? Am I afraid to seek you in my soul, lest finding You I must give up all else? I am certainly a strange, complex human being who seeks love and runs away from it at the same time. It is like being offered billions of dollars and being content with a penny, like starving but refusing to eat. . . . Do not permit me, dear Lord, to live so close to Heaven and be so totally unaware of it, to be so close to peace and live in turmoil, to be immersed in the furnace of love and refuse to change. Grant that my soul may be as wax in Your hands, pliable enough to mold into Your image, Lord and Savior.

A PRAYER TO TRUST DIVINE PROVIDENCE

My Jesus, give me perception. It is so easy to get caught up in material things and in everyday cares. Sometimes these seemingly necessary concerns choke Your Word in my soul and I am unable to see the right course to take. One day You reprimanded Your Apostles because they were concerned about food and forgot how You had fed them and let them want for nothing. It must hurt Your generous Heart when I doubt Your Providence or forget Your past gifts to me. If You have taken care in the past, why do I doubt that You will continue to do so in the future? You are changeless and Your Goodness is not dependent upon my goodness. You are always good and provident and I must never worry about tomorrow nor doubt Your continuing Providence. I must keep in mind that Your Providence rises before the dawn and never sleeps at sunset. You are a faithful God Who straightens any crooked ways before I ever set foot on them.

Prayer should be the means by which I, at all times, receive all that I need, and, for this reason, be my daily refuge, my daily consolation, my daily joy, my source of rich and inexhaustible joy in life.

—*St. John Chrysostom*

During Sickness

PRAYER FOR THE SICK

This prayer was composed by St. Peter Fourier and was included in the PCPA Prayer Book. Given Mother Angelica's incessant illnesses as a novice and junior professed, it was no doubt often on her lips. Following are some of her own pleas to God, written during Mother's physical sufferings.

Come, O Jesus, to complement Thy pains in me and to fill up what is lacking of Thy sufferings.

—Colossians 1:24

I offer Thee my body, that Thou mayest impress thereon, through Thy Spirit, all that is pleasing to Thee. Were it possible for me to offer Thee as many bodies as I have limbs, gladly would I do so with all my heart. Therefore, I pray Thee, O my sovereign Good, my only Love, to increase my pains according to Thy good pleasure and to prolong my sufferings as Thou willest. My miserable body I surrender to Thee for the infliction of as manifold pains as there are unfaithful souls who refuse to suffer according to Thy spirit. O my All, willingly shall I endure tortures from all my fellow men. Accept my offering and bestow on me Thy Spirit. I desire nothing but Thee alone, my sweetest Lord Jesus Christ. I surrender myself as a victim to Thee, not because I am worthy of this grace or deserve this privilege, but because through us Thou art pleased to suffer here below for the honor of Thy Father. Amen. (PCPA Prayer Book)

DURING AN ILLNESS

I feel sick today, dear Jesus, my head throbs and my body is so weak it is an effort to even talk to You. I try to think of Your poor head when it was crowned with thorns and I marvel at Your fortitude. I think of how very weak You must have been when You took the Cross upon Your shoulders. I marvel at Your Love. Love was the driving power that made You strong when You were weak. If I could just remember Your Love was for *me*. You suffered for *me!* Well then, I will do the same for You. It is strange, dear Jesus, that as soon as I think of Your pain, mine seems slight.

OFFERING OF PAIN

Suffering Jesus, I unite my pain with all the pain You suffered on the Cross. I do not understand the mystery of pain. I do not grasp the power contained within it—power to change a stubborn will into a docile will, power to change frustration into patient serenity, power to mold a finite soul into a beautiful masterpiece for the Father to behold. Ah yes, my Jesus, I do not understand but I do believe in its power because it formed such a large portion of Your earthly life and was used to redeem mankind. My human nature rebels against pain. My reason tells me it is unnecessary, but my heart tells me that without it, in one form or another, I shall never possess the wedding garment so necessary for the Kingdom. Help me to comprehend the mysterious and hidden power of all the suffering that molds my soul into Your Image, Lord Jesus.

PRAYER FOR COURAGE IN PAIN

Your Goodness, O Jesus, provide for all Your creatures and yet You had to depend on someone to provide for You. How very much You love me! Love is proven by Sacrifice and You have proven Your Love for me. This realization makes me feel small for I am forced to admit that my love for You is very little. I run from sacrifice and I am afraid of pain. Death at times seems like a dark tunnel to be traveled, and the future seems bleak. When I compare my attitude with Yours I realize that in myself I have nothing to offer You. The only claim I have is Your Love for me. When I think of that Love I feel a sudden surge of courage to face the future. Even death becomes merely the beautiful moment when the One who loves and the one who is loved meet face-to-face.

A CRY OF DEPENDENCE

Lord Father, life is always easier when I keep close to You. Sometimes I wonder why it is so hard to keep my soul united to the only Source of happiness. It would seem that I should be drawn to You like a piece of iron to a magnet and yet my own will and frailties form a barrier which keeps my soul separated from You. The very thing I want to be, I am not. I run away from the pruning I need in order be like You. My life is such a contradiction. My soul yearns for holiness and then runs from the mortification necessary to attain it. I shall have to depend on You, dear Jesus, to lift my poor soul out of its weakness and clothe it with the courage and strength of Your Holy Spirit. Then You will bear fruit in me—fruit pleasing to the Father.

Prayers of the Past, Present, and Future

At the center of Mother Angelica's spirituality is her call to "live in the Present Moment." Inspired by the teachings of Brother Lawrence, Mother Angelica taught that we must shake off the bondage of the past, free ourselves of the cares of the future, and live fully in this present moment, responding to God's Will in it. The following three prayers by Mother will help you get there.

HEALING WHAT IS PAST

Father, I enter into Your Compassionate Spirit and try to drink deeply of Your Merciful Love. My memory smarts with the remembrance of past offenses and my soul is pained by the anger of yesterdays—days in the past that bring tears and sadness. Every time I think they are gone they return with renewed vigor and I realize I have not grown in compassion and forgiveness. I put my memory into Your Compassionate Mercy, Lord and Father, and I ask You to cover its wounds with the healing balm of Your Mercy. Let my soul sink deep into that fathomless ocean of Mercy and return to me renewed, healed, and refreshed, with love for everyone and malice toward none.

PRAYER FOR THIS PRESENT TIME

Life is so short, my Lord. I look at all my yesterdays and they seem so hazy while all my tomorrows are uncertain. The only time I really possess is this tiny moment and it passes so quickly. Why does time weigh so heavily in my life? It is a most precious gift from Your hands and I should look at it as I would a treasure. It provides the opportunity for me to know You better and love you more, to become like Jesus and be filled with Your own Spirit, to increase in holiness and to make reparation for my sins. Thank You, my Lord, for time. Please grant me more time to love You and tell You how very sorry I am for ever having offended You.

PRAYER FOR CONFIDENCE IN THE FUTURE

Lord Spirit, fear of the future fills my soul and I realize how little I trust You. Your Power created the universe and Your Providence takes care of the birds in the air, the fish in the sea, and the tiniest insect. How much more will You take care of me. Does my fear stem from attachment, Lord? Tell me, my dearest Friend and Guide, tell me what is the root of my fears? What prevents me from possessing that love which casts out fear and that confidence which overcomes every obstacle?

To the Holy Spirit

FOR THE INSPIRATIONS OF THE HOLY SPIRIT

Holy Spirit, I am sorry for ignoring the many inspirations You have given me. The Father and Jesus sent You to sanctify me. I know You plan, guide, and arrange everything in my life for the good of my soul and yet when things do not go my way, or pain is my portion, I wonder where You are. My selfishness makes me desire the consolation of Your Presence and Your Gifts. My soul rebels at the thought of the dryness that makes me strong and the suffering that transforms me into Jesus. I complain that You do not speak to me and yet I ignore every good inspiration that Your Voice plants in my mind. My pride makes me think that every good thought is my own. I forget that I could not say "Jesus is Lord" unless Your Voice first whispered it into my ear. Free my soul, Holy Spirit, of the cares of this world and from myself so I may hear Your Voice clearly and my soul may follow Your inspirations with alacrity and docility. I want You to guide and direct every moment of my life that I may hear Your Voice and return love for love.

Prayer for the Seven Gifts of the Holy Spirit

First Gift: Fear of the Lord

Holy Spirit, Jesus said that His Father was also *Our* Father. Teach me what it means to know that He is *my* Father. I have a tendency to look at Him as Father of the human race by reason of His Creative Power. That is very general and somehow it doesn't seem to be what Jesus meant. He told Mary Magdalene that God was *her* Father and so He is also mine — all mine. If I could only remember that truth: The Creator of the Universe — Great, Majestic, Glorious — is *my* Father! He looks upon me as His child, cares about me, and loves me. Give me a childlike, loving fear of ever offending such a Father. Let my life console Him and grant that I may ever please Him.

Second Gift: Piety

Holy Spirit, Jesus gave us a New Commandment — to love one another as much as He loves us. I find it difficult to love that much. Some people are so unlovable and others are sometimes unjust and cruel. How can I love like Jesus unless You, Lord Spirit, come and love through me? Somehow, down deep in my soul I know that the only way to love anyone is the way Jesus loves them. When I love as my human heart dictates then my love goes from on to off and hot to cold. I'm forever on a seesaw, loving some often and others seldom. My emotions go up and down like a thermometer and loving becomes either drudgery or ecstasy. How selfish it is to love only few.

Do I find it difficult because I love only those who render me a service, Lord Spirit? Is the secret of loving like Jesus to love just for love itself, expecting no return? I am forced to admit that Jesus loves unselfishly. He loves because He is Good; He loves because He is Love itself. His Love is gratuitous and my love is all mixed up with myself. I come first and my neighbor second. Lord Spirit, pour love—real love—into my heart. Take out my earthly heart and replace it with a spiritual heart—a heart free of all selfish motives—a heart that can do nothing but love—a heart that knows no greed, or selfishness, or lukewarmness, or coldness. Most of all, let it be a forgiving heart, an all-embracing heart—a heart that is content only when it is doing the one thing it was created to do—pump life-giving love into all men.

Third Gift: Fortitude

Holy Spirit, give me courage for today—courage to be a Christian. It is so easy to compromise with the world—to have a little of You and a little of the world—to be comfortable with just a little of both. I know that everything this world has to offer is passing, but I cling to it. Is it because everything here gives the appearance of being real and solid? This is not true. A wind can destroy the most solid object. Water can rot the most beautiful wood. Fire can turn buildings into ashes. People die and their bodies decay. What is real and solid about all that? You know, Lord Spirit, it takes great courage to keep that in mind and not despair! It is hard to face the truth and though I often desire to face reality, when that reality faces me, I run.

To have courage I need trust—trust in Your Strength in me. I need to recall that You see everything and Your Grace is always there the moment I need it—not a second before. Fear and cowardice come from a lack of trust, from self-pity and inferiority. Help me, Lord Spirit, to do whatever task is presented to me by Your Providence with joy and assurance— assurance that success will be mine with Your Grace and self-knowledge will be mine with failure. Never let me forget that You stand by me no matter what happens because You love me.

Fourth Gift: Counsel

Holy Spirit, I find it hard to know Your Will in my life. I know from past experience, the fact that I desire something does not necessarily indicate it is Your Will. Sometimes what I desire is opposed to Your Will but somehow I manage to talk myself into believing You want it. How do I discern between divine inspiration and the desires of my own heart? Give me light, Lord, to see the ultimate fruit of every decision. If the fruit is good, give me courage to accomplish it no matter how difficult. If the fruit is bad, give me even more courage to choose another course. Give me that special intuition that will awaken my conscience in the presence of evil so I may never permit myself to be put into dangerous situations. Let me know, Lord, that love makes all things possible and that Love is the backbone of courage, for love casts out fear and trepidation. Give me the simplicity of a child and the courage of a warrior. Let my soul be so attuned to Your Will that You have only to pluck the strings of desire and I will play the song of love on the violin of life. I praise the Wisdom that directs me with such prudence and love and then rewards me for following a perfect course. Help me to see, Lord, that Your Way and Your Will are always better than my own.

Fifth Gift: Knowledge

Holy Spirit, I desire knowledge but not the knowledge of things or of this world. This kind of knowledge will pass. I want to know You—Your ways—Your love—and most of all, I want to know the one thing necessary. I want to do my best at the work You have given me but I want to be detached from that work. It is so hard to be enthusiastic about something without becoming attached.

Enthusiasm seems to encourage possession and then I become a slave to a thing or a cause. If I could only put my heart into everything just because I see You in it, Your honor or Your growth in my neighbor. If only my motives were more spiritual and unselfish, I would not run the danger of becoming attached or possessing a wrong set of values. My heart would be free to love much and do much without danger. I would not be thinking of myself or how much I accomplish. I would be free of the burden of carrying my opinions and desires around like a bag of toys.

Lord, if I could see the spiritual value of my moment-to-moment existence, it would give me a clear vision of its relationship to You and the Kingdom. My life would not be shallow but filled to overflowing with the Knowledge that comes from You. Time would become a treasure box containing a multitude of precious jewels—jewels that I would find in the Kingdom—pearls of great price whose value would be known only to You.

Sixth Gift: Understanding

Lord, give me a spirit of prayer. I want my soul to be like a sponge that soaks up the water of divine grace contained in every moment of life. I would like to begin my Heaven now, not by an absence of suffering, but by a continuous union with You. I would like my heart to be attuned to Your Presence in creation, in life situations, in my neighbor, and in my own soul. I would like to hear the silence of Your Presence in the noise of this world. I would like the ability to find You when You decide to play hide-and-seek with my soul; and when I find You, hold on tight until You must leave again lest I love Your gifts more than You. I would like to understand the Scriptures and see within them all those mysteries reserved for the simple and childlike—the mysteries that are hidden from the wise and prudent. I would like to be able to penetrate the mysteries of life, not for the sake of knowledge but just to see Your Beautiful Attributes in a variety of ways. I would like to see You in every human being I meet and reach out to each in love and compassion. O God, I guess what I'm trying to say is that I love You and I desire that every moment of my life I may grow in that love by ever being aware of Your Presence in season and out of season, in rain and sunshine, in joy and sorrow, in the visible and invisible realities.

Seventh Gift: Wisdom

Holy Spirit, give me the kind of Wisdom that is Yours. I do not think the way You think and my human ways are not Your ways. Your Wisdom is so far beyond mine. Your Wisdom says that the peaceful, meek, poor in spirit, and those who mourn are blessed. Your Wisdom says that I should dance for joy when people abuse me or persecute me for the name and cause of Jesus. Your Wisdom says that if I die to myself in this life I shall bear much fruit and give glory to the Father. Your Wisdom chose suffering and the Cross by which to redeem men. You chose the very thing that was considered a curse—to remove a curse. Your Wisdom chose twelve uneducated laymen to build Your Church—a mustard seed that had to suffer itself before beginning to bear the fruit of many conversions. Your Wisdom chose the path of martyrdom to spread the Good News far and wide. Your Wisdom brings good out of evil instead of preventing evil. Truly, my Lord, Your Wisdom is different from mine. Unless I see things in the light You see them, I will live in a world of pretend—a life of make-believe—a dream world in which I try to make things the way I want them and become frustrated when I don't succeed. My wisdom needs everything almost perfect before it can improve upon it, or else changes it so drastically that it no longer exists as it was. My wisdom cannot reap the fruit of every life situation, every pain, and every heartache. My wisdom sees only the exterior and does not go beyond. My lack of penetration into the core of everything makes my views narrow and my opinions set. O Lord God, give me the wisdom to see with spiritual eyes the invisible values in every sorrow and pain. Help me to see Your Face in the destitute, Your Plan in the world, Your Love guiding my life, our power in creation. Help me go beyond what appears and see that invisible Providence that guides all things to good and rules with a mighty Hand. I want to be aware of Your Divine Arms around me, protecting me from untold harm. I want to know with an unexplainable intuition the length and depth of Your Divine Love for me. I want my days to be filled with Your Love and my nights with Your Peace. Let my walking be in Your Paths and my sleeping in Your Arms. I want my mind to be like a river flowing with the clear water of Your Inspiration and my heart a reservoir never empty of Your Grace. I want You, O God, and then I shall possess all the things that Wisdom is, and my soul shall rest secure in the Arms of Omnipotence.

> Virtues are formed by prayer.
> Prayer preserves temperance.
> Prayer suppresses anger.
> Prayer prevents emotions of pride and envy.
> Prayer draws into the soul the Holy Spirit, and
> raises man to Heaven.
>
> —*St. Ephraem*

The Dark Night

PRAYER FOR SELF-CONTROL

Holy Spirit, I find self-control so difficult at times. When I feel angry it is so justified in my mind that I cannot control the bitterness and resentment that overpowers me. It is the same with impatience. I never seem to be at fault. My impatience becomes justified and yet my inner self tells me that this is not so. Every day I make resolutions to be moderate in eating and in this, too, I fail. I need that special quality of soul and strengthening of will that would enable me to say no to myself and all these weaknesses that clamor for control of my will. I desire, Holy Spirit, to be so aware of Jesus at every moment of my life that I will act like Him in every circumstance and have the self-control that is the fruit of peace and love. Let me bear this fruit in my soul that I may glorify the Father.

PRAYER FOR GRACES FROM
THE MOTHER OF GOD

Sweet Mother, give me the graces I need for this day. Let me be open to all the graces you have in store for me; the graces you know I need, even those I do not know I need.

MOTHER ANGELICA'S PRAYERS DURING A DARK NIGHT OF THE SOUL

By the summer of 1984, Mother Angelica had lost her birth mother, Mae Rizzo (later, Sr. Mary David), her network EWTN was in financial turmoil, and two competing Catholic networks had risen to challenge her. These crushing events and more threw Mother into a "Dark Night of the Soul" experience between July and October of that year. A fuller understanding of the events surrounding this spiritual struggle can be found in Chapter 12 of my biography Mother Angelica: The Remarkable Story of a Nun, Her Nerve, and a Network of Miracles. *For the first time in her religious life Mother kept a prayer journal, a record of her desolation. To the outside world, nothing appeared out of order. As Mother fulfilled her television commitments and led her community with her usual aplomb, the world was oblivious to the darkness enveloping her. Interiorly she was plagued by doubts and lost in spiritual anguish. Here, for the first time, is her complete "Dark Night" diary. It is hard reading. In it she wrestles with her failure to love Christ, the impermanence of the world, and her personal failings. It reads like a long, slow spiritual descent into darkness. May Mother's heartfelt cries from the abyss give those in similar straits hope and comfort.*

Never was fount so clear,
undimmed and bright;
From it alone, I know proceeds all light
although 'tis night.

—St. John of the Cross

July 7, 1984

My Lord and God, this morning I came to You and asked You how to love. There are so many to love—they are all so different. My soul cried out in anguish, "Teach me how to love." Then You spoke to me and said, "Enter into Me and see with My Eyes, love with My Heart, speak words of comfort with My Voice." My heart overflowed and it was as if a great light burst around me. Everyone who came into my path I could see with Your Eyes and Your Love poured out to them. Then Lord, unbelievable darkness enveloped me. It was as if people from every corner came into view. There were so many. I seemed so small, so empty, so alone. My soul seemed suddenly drained of every ounce of love. My capacity to love was shattered, my strength overcome by weakness. Everyone I love was snatched away from me by some unknown force and I stood before You, Lord God, broken; alone and empty. I groped in the darkness feeling for Your Hand, but It kept eluding me. And then all hell broke loose and near despair surrounded me. It seemed I was incapable of loving anyone. My love was selfish and self-centered. What everyone thought I possessed I did not, so I thought I must be a hypocrite. All the demands made upon me were impossible to fulfill.

Then a chasm opened up before me and I knew my place forever if I did not love. I stood petrified with fear unable to squeeze out the least bit of love. I cried out for someone to love me, thinking I would then have something to give. But there was no one. The ones I always felt loved me were nowhere to be seen, they were gone. I looked right and left but the only ones I could see were those who needed me: the lonely, the sick, those who live in vacuums, friends and enemies, children, and the elderly. Everyone looked to me with pleading eyes. My hands were empty, my soul dried up. I looked in vain for a corner of the earth to give me respite and refreshment but there was none. Was there no place to run, no one to understand, no one to tell the truth? I said, "I am empty. You see, I have nothing to give." But it was useless. They all kept looking, pleading for love, His love in me.

"Lord God, my soul stands between total darkness and nothingness. I cry out to You to teach me how to love. Fill me, for I have nothing of my own to give." Do I hear Your voice tell me I will never have anything of my own to give? Yes, I know it is true. I must love only with Your love in me. I must live as if no one loved me in return. I must love with such a pure love that there is no love in me at all except Your love. Any love I receive from anyone is Your love manifest through my neighbor. My heart feels suspended between heaven and earth as I feebly make my way on the path You have walked: the Cross of Love. Pour into this empty shell whatever is needed by others in the present moment. When I feel alone, let me comfort others. When I am disheartened, let me give comfort. When my heart is broken, let me heal the brokenness of others. Though I lose all possessions, let me continue to give from my poverty of spirit. Though I am stripped of the clothing of others' love, let me place a warm mantle of love around the destitute, the lonely and disheartened. I have asked You how to love and You have exposed my emptiness. Fill me with Your life, love, and Presence for I have nothing of myself to give. I have no source of love but You. It is You who must give and You who must receive in me.

JULY 8, 1984

There is in me today the hollowness of a drum. People and things bounce off of me. As I reach out to grasp them they are too far away. I look around for the sight of Your Face, but You too are far away. I shall wait as one who serves. My eyes look for You. My being cries out to You. Teach me how to love. I shall not grasp, I shall only wait.

JULY 9, 1984

My soul feels separated from my body. . . . Am I called to live and yet be so detached that I am alone in the midst of many? Am I somehow to be suspended so the breath of Your Spirit can move me to and fro?

My Lord, truly it was not men who crucified You, it was love. You were nailed to a cross loving with a burning heart but unable at that moment to receive love in return. Your Mother and John's sorrowful love only increased Your pain. The two people You loved the most, Your Mother and John, were both standing at the foot of the Cross but still You uttered the cry of abandonment. You emptied Yourself so totally. Are You asking me to do the same? I am afraid. It seems like a living death. I do not possess the strength. Help me, Oh God.

JULY 10, 1984

The struggle continues, my Lord. Am I fighting against whatever You are trying to do in my soul? . . . I cling to everything and as I do I feel it slip through my fingers. What or who is there that will not pass from me sooner or later, anyway? Is not everything like the grass that is seen today and gone tomorrow?

Am I getting a glimpse of what You are asking, my Lord? Am I to be so absorbed in Your Presence, in Your Love that my human love, my desires, my feelings, and needs disappear and are swallowed up in Your Presence? How can this be done? My weakness blocks the vision of Your Face. My struggles push away the inner longings of my soul. My sins loom up as many phantoms of the night to haunt me and make me step back from your awesome Holiness.

JULY 10, 1984, NOON

I am helpless, oh God. Everything around me seems to be falling apart. Everything I hold dear is getting farther and farther away. Gentle Jesus, have mercy on me.

JULY 11, 1984

I know, my Lord, that you wish me to be a vehicle of Your Love, but my poor human nature recoils from the selflessness so necessary to be a fit instrument in Your Hands. Your faithful son, St. John of the Cross, said, "All and nothing." Is this my portion? You are King of Kings and Lord of Lords. You are Savior and Redeemer. You are Powerful and Majestic. Is not Your love enough for me? Why do I fear being alone? Is it because in my small mind there are still two of us instead of one of us in union of heart, mind, and soul? You told Your followers that You only did what You saw the Father do and You only said what You heard the Father say. You only did His Will. That was Your food. Is this my way? Shall my being become so one with You as You are in the Father? I am frightened at the purity of love so necessary for that kind of union. I feel helpless. I cling to the plastic toys we call possessions. How terrible. I must admit I chose the flickering light of a match instead of the brilliant light of Your Presence. Your Mercy, oh God, is so great. You pursue me and I run. You seek me and I hide. You hem me in and I rebel. You love me. Teach me how to love.

JULY 12, 1984

I realized in the early hours of this day—it is You, oh Lord—I do not know how to love. I have tried to do Your Will. I have kept Your Commandments. What is wanting in my love? "Give all" You say, "give Me even your desires; your desires for yourself, your loved ones, your work, your community. Give everything and everyone to Me. You take care of Me and I will take care of them. I call You to holiness that is total, that I alone may live in you. There are many cares in your soul. Give them to Me. I need your love to comfort Me. Let us live alone together and every desire of your heart shall be fulfilled.

Those who see you will see Me because we will be one in mind and heart. What I take from you, I take only for your good. Seek your losses in My Arms and I will place all your problems in the furnace of My burning Love."

. . . In my effort, oh Lord, to be like You have I concentrated too much on how to love others and forgotten that the only love in me that is powerful enough to help my neighbor is Your Love? It is Your Love that must overflow and manifest itself in compassion, kindness, forgiveness, and mercy. How can I possibly see with Your Eyes and speak with Your Words if Your Love is not burning within me?

JULY 13, 1984

Your Presence surrounds me like a cloak. I am aware of that Other Presence as I go about my duties. You are quiet, My Lord, serene and lovingly looking out from my soul as from the top of a mountain, with Eyes forward and Eyes upward. You never lose sight of Your Father. You never lose sight of me. You always seek my neighbor to love in me. The things of this world are as the breath of air — coming and going before. Your Presence comforts me as it sears me — purifies me. It is always at work changing, depriving, enveloping, soothing, chastising, and caressing.

JULY 14, 1984

Once again everything seems to be slipping away. I stand before You without support, as one who is stripped of every possession, every desire. My soul is at times flung to the heavens by the overflowing of Your Presence and dashed to the earth as one discarded and of little value. Shall there ever be a time when my will and Your Will will be so one that my peace will remain steadfast? Just when I feel in control, detached, and totally Yours, my soul is torn open by Your Light in the circumstances around me and I am aghast at my weakness, appalled by my lack of love and union.

JULY 15, 1984

Lord, is there no end to the searing light of Your Love? The tiniest affection or possession looms before me at times and I can see the slightest tinge of selfishness harboring within. It distresses me beyond words. As I draw close to embrace it, I turn around instead to hand it over to You. It is as if an invisible force draws everything within me out into an empty space where I only observe from afar—knowing it was mine and now it is Yours. Have I lost everything? Is it not all much better in Your Heart than mine!

JULY 16, 1984

What is this strange feeling of losing and receiving? I feel called to leave all things, all those I love, and myself, so You can reign supreme. But instead my nature continues to push and pull, give and take back, aspire to the heights and cling to the earth from which it came. I reach out to the All as I hold fast to earth. What madness is this? Do I suffer from illusions? Are the heights beyond me? No, it cannot be so. Your Arms are always outstretched on the Cross. I look at You, Lord

Jesus, in such agony and wonder. I see You as One who loves with an infinite love—as One who is totally united to the Father in Love and yet You suffer from the lack of love from me, from Your chosen ones, from mankind. Is this not a paradox, my Jesus: that You love the Father, You do only His Will and yet You suffer from my lack of love, my lukewarmness, my lack of a quick response. My Jesus, is there something I do not see? Am I missing an element of love? What is detachment when it is possible for You, the Lord of Lords, to Love the Father so deeply and yet suffer from lack of love from finite creatures? I thought detached love meant one was so wrapped in God that one did not care, or see or need any other love, any other possession, any other thing of this earth.

But You, oh Jesus, lived and died in total poverty, Your Will stripped of any desire except to accomplish the Father's Will. Yes, still in the midst of such Love You felt keenly that You came unto Your own and Your own did not receive You. Why, when You possessed such Love did You feel the pain of the indifference of your creatures? You showed St. Margaret Mary Your wounded Heart, a Heart in love with mankind and so little loved in return. Why so many thorns, tiny, piercing thorns around so much love? Why doesn't the burning furnace of Love that is within Your Heart consume the thorns, wipe away the wounds, soothe the pain?

JULY 17, 1984

Teach me, oh Jesus, the secret of Love—teach me how to love. Open to me the door of Your Heart that my love may be intense enough to be like Yours, human enough to feel the thorns, vulnerable enough not to fear the pain. My Jesus, You are God and man. As God, You have need of no one. As man, You long for my love. As God-man You seek only my good. You wait as I search. You long for my expressions of love for You. You endure the pain of waiting for me to see Your Face in everything. You wait at the door of my heart and knock and yet Your Love for the Father is Infinite, total.

JULY 18, 1984

It seems the more intense Your Love, the more it seeks to love that which is human and weak. My soul is troubled as I ponder this mystery. I always felt and thought that if I love You intensely I would not be affected by the presence or absence of human love, possessions, success, and all those things in daily life that make it livable and bearable. As I ponder Your Life, my Jesus, You loved the Father and did everything only in Him, through Him and with Him accomplishing His Will in everything. Yet I find You crying over Jerusalem, asking Peter if he loved You more than the others, crying with Martha and Mary, feeling shunned at the Pharisees banquet, wondering why the nine lepers do not return and give You thanks, crushed over Judas, and disappointed in Peter. How does it all blend together, my Jesus?

Is it the giving and not receiving that gave You such pain? Were there times You gave and received, and it still caused You pain? Yes, it must be so. When You met Your Mother on the way of the Cross, what pain Your mutual love caused You.

Even before that, to see Your Mother so poor, Your Disciples misunderstanding Your Message—always looking for the glory of this world, seeing John and Your Mother standing so sorrowful beneath the Cross. Yes, it seems, my Lord, that to love as You loved in this life is to be open, vulnerable, ready to love so intensely that one's heart ceaselessly gives as an overflowing fountain, vulnerable enough to feel the least absence of love but generous enough to stand beneath the cross of separation, misunderstanding, hostility, and loneliness and never closing the floodgates of love. Is it to be able to feel the numbness of heartache and never surrender to self-pity, to long and thirst for infinite Love and struggle with the attachments that seem so much a part of us?

I desire to be absorbed and surrounded with Infinite Light and yet somehow am content with the light of a small candle.

JULY 19, 1984

Where am I, oh God! Be merciful! Bathe me in Your Mercy, clothe me with compassion. Be my shield in the midst of this battle. Be my Light in the midst of this darkness. Do not abandon me to myself. I shall run to Mary and hide in her Immaculate Heart.

JULY 20, 1984

Today I feel a terrible pull. It is as if Love was coming into my heart and leaving it with such force that I must somehow hold my breath in an effort to hold on to some of it. It is as if everyone and everything I love is at times safely tucked away in my heart and then I see each one, each thing slowly being withdrawn to leave me gasping for a love that is constant, unchanging, always the same.

JULY 21, 1984

Today it is as if I am looking through a mist—a spiritual mist. Faintly I see all those I love and all the things around me. They pass by one by one and I do not grasp for them. I do not draw them to myself. I do not clasp them to my heart. They remain figures through the mist as I stand still looking and waiting— for what, I do not know.

I am alone. There is a Presence in this mist. It is between and around everything I see. I am lonely but peaceful. There is no noise. There is a silence. I seem separated from them and yet somehow among them. There are times I sense I desire to draw away as if my poor human nature was still rebelling against some force or some change in my life. Exactly what do I fear? I remember the Hound of Heaven and wonder. I act more loving to everyone as my heart feels more distant. I feel somehow I do not belong. I am in a foreign land. The language I want to share no one understands. The trials I undergo I cannot express.

JULY 22, 1984

There is around me a quiet Presence and at the same time a sense of loss; a sense of being emptied of everything, of being stripped of my very self. Everything looks so plastic, so small, so insignificant. His Presence stands by, but does not yet fill me. He looks on quietly, loving, present—and then hidden. I see Him standing, waiting. I want to run to Him but I cannot. What is it I must shed? What is it that I must sacrifice? What part of me is still not totally His? I am tired and weary—I plead and pray—I seek and knock—I cry out and there is no answer—it is so quiet. There is a hope-filled separation between He and I. He looks at me with great love. His Eyes pierce my soul and yet I cannot run into His Embrace. His Love beckons but I am unable to move forward. I feel pulled from behind by another force and although I strive to move forward I am unable to do so. I pray for grace to correspond. I pray for hope for I do not see progress as an end to this trial. Will I cross over the invisible wall that stands between us? I wonder if my own selfishness is the wall. He stands silently loving as if I am to make some decision.

Feelings of fear and rebellion flow over my soul like waves on the shoreline and I become disheartened. I am unable to do what He asks even though my soul longs for union with Jesus. How long will He wait? How long will I be unsure—or am I sure and do not wish to make the sacrifice? I wonder if the sacrifices He asks would be as painful as the agony I feel in this uncertainty. "Be patient with me, Lord. Show me the path You trod and give me the grace to follow in Your footsteps."

JULY 23, 1984

I see something I did not see before or did I not want to see it? I see, My Lord, that I am to love with Your Love and Your

Love alone. I must allow You and You alone to receive all the Love that comes to me but my human nature may never allow any of that love that comes from my neighbor to distract me from you. My being is to be used by You, Lord God, as a vehicle of love for You alone: You to give, You to receive.

JULY 26, 1984

My soul is in such turmoil. My imperfections and weaknesses seem to be bursting within me and exploding on every side. I fight for the least good thought. I struggle to pray. Every prayer is separated by tons of aggravating thoughts, turmoil, and distress. It is like picking roses amidst a garbage heap.

My world seems to have fallen apart—I am devastated—I am alone in the midst of many. I am desolate in the midst of those who love me. I am abandoned in the midst of loving friends. So many say they love me, and yet my soul stands by and feels only a cold wind that dissipates all the warmth that comes from the words "I love You."

If I am called to love as He loves I am indeed the poorest of all creatures, for of myself I have nothing to give. Nothing.

A trial came today. I wept without control. My soul was torn asunder by my lack of union with His Will. My soul seemed to sway within my body as for one who died. Is this, oh God, what You call me to: a spiritual death? Am I to live in this world as one who died to it? How can I manifest compassion and love if I feel so dead inside?

JULY 28, 1984

You have given me a light, oh Lord, and I look upon it in awe and trembling. I realize the many weaknesses I possess that prevent me from loving as You love. My weaknesses put up barriers so I am not able to respond to everyone with the same love. The faults of some repel me, while the virtues of others attract me. As a result my heart, mind, and actions are on a yo-yo. I am then angered by faults in others and my love for them is diminished. This weakness in me now brings intolerable pain, for I see Your Love and the comparison is so great it causes me pain beyond words. I seem so helpless. My desire to be like You grows, but I am unable to change. I seem to be standing still.

Your Love is greater than anyone's sins, faults, and weaknesses. My love stops or at least is impeded by the smart of sins and weaknesses. My love is on the same level as that of my neighbor; it has not risen above them, it has not reached that place where it is fed by You alone and then flows out to my neighbor regardless of his effect on me. How do I rise above, oh God?

JULY 29, 1984

Do I see a glimmer of light, my Lord, as to what my role is: my way of loving as You love? Am I to live as You lived? Loved as You loved Your Apostles? Seemingly loving some with a love of preference and special mission, having compassion on the multitudes? And yet with all this there was in You aloneness. Your human nature was forced at times to withdraw so You could be alone with the Father. Do I sense that as You walked the earth, loved Your people, forgave their sins, and healed their ills there was always that union with the Father so great that You could warn us that we do not "have here a lasting city," that "we seek first the Kingdom and all these other things would be added"? Was Your loneliness for the Father? [Was it] union with the Father in Your human nature that allowed you to say "I only say what I hear the Father say. I only do what I see the Father do"? Oh, blessed aloneness that keeps me at the door of Your Heart, as I take from Your Open Side the love to love with; the compassion to have mercy with; and the courage to give without counting the cost. Is this loneliness not the key to union with You, my Jesus? I feel somehow like I am between heaven and earth. I long for more union—more love from You—and as I reach high and the distance seems so great, Your Love flows through me to my neighbor giving him whatever he needs as I stand alone between heaven and earth my arms outstretched to touch You, my eyes riveted on Your Face.

The Light is brighter and I blindly push forward to what is too bright for me to see. The Light creates a darkness that seems to be my shield so I may continue my journey toward the Light in safety. Are faith and blessed loneliness the two hands I clasp during my journey? Do they keep me from stumbling? Are they somehow united to the Light that keeps me on course so I do not turn back? My being looks to Thee alone, my weaknesses are swallowed up in the brightness.

There is an abandon that is mixed with the loneliness — it is like a cement that keeps the loneliness from seeking itself in the things of earth. Abandonment and loneliness seem to blend to keep me going toward the Light, trusting those behind me and around me to His Love. The Light pulls all of them toward Itself.

JULY 30, 1984

My Lord, Your Light blinds me at times, soothes me at other times, and corrects me when I choose the wrong path. Keep my eyes on Your Light. Let the hand of Faith guide me through the darkness and the hand of Grace guide me through the loneliness that grows so intense every moment.

JULY 31, 1984

My Lord, my soul is filled with the desire to keep my eyes on Your Light. It is as if my soul was standing between heaven and earth. I see Your Spirit as a Light that is so bright, but it does not blind. My arms reach out to You in supplication for all mankind. I feel a desire to love them all. As Your Love penetrates my being I realize that suddenly all those I love have become dearer to me. It is as if I was able to love them totally and without reserve. Your Love penetrates and goes through me to them. Detachment is no longer frightening. It is not an absence of love, it is not indifference, it is to penetrate Your Love more and more so that the love I possess for others is more pure, more intense, more unselfish, more attuned to their needs rather than mine. Let my love then always rise above human frailties and imperfections. Let it be centered in You so completely that the love I love with will be like Your Love for the Father. Have I learned too late? No Lord, a moment of pure love would be worth a lifetime of selfish love.

As I walk today, dear Jesus, let my eyes keep themselves on Thee. In the midst of business, confusion, and the things of the world Your Will has placed before me, let me never for a moment forget what you wish of me: to be Love as You are Love. Your Light envelops me. Your Presence beckons me to the one thing necessary: to know Thee, love Thee, and serve Thee with every fiber of my being.

AUGUST 1, 1984

As I go my way everything around me is like cardboard in comparison to the Light my soul beholds. I try to keep my gaze upon it. When my duties take possession of my thought it is as if the Light rests in my heart. I am aware of It though my eyes are not upon it. My soul seems to be in a constant attitude of supplication when it gazes upon the Light. It is a fragile gift. I feel I must somehow be very careful not to be disturbed. There is a silent power in the Light that overwhelms the earthenware jar that stands before It.

AUGUST 11, 1984

I feel I must somehow be completely empty. I am aware that the Light desires me to enter into It, but I cannot. I stand in front of It, unable to be empty enough to walk through and rest within It. I feel my neighbor is somehow being deprived of more love from me because I am still not totally one with the Light I gaze upon. I seem so helpless to overcome those weaknesses that I feel keep me back. No matter how much I try, they have some strong hold on me.

I look at the Light with great longing but some invisible bonds hold me tight and I cannot move. It is bittersweet. The Light gives me joy. The inability to run into It causes me agony of soul. Is this like purgatory? What joyful pain must reign there!

AUGUST 25, 1984

I am aware of the Light before me.

OCTOBER 22, 1984

I feel as if I have been thrown down into a pit. My weaknesses overwhelm me. I find in my soul such deep tendencies to all kinds of sins that I feel God looks upon my soul as some wretched, finite being who has been ungrateful for His Love and Grace. I am steeped in self and my soul cries out for deliverance from this torment. Oh, God, You know my heart. My eyes constantly fill with tears and I know not why. I cry out to You and You do not hear. But I shall trust in Your mercy. I am nothingness. You alone are all. I am who am not. You are the great "I AM." If the knowledge of my weaknesses pleases You, if my soul being crushed to powder is to Your Honor and Glory, then Your Will be done. I have disappointed

You and I'm sorry. I have been unfaithful to Your Grace and Love. How can I desire to love as You love, oh God, when I am wretchedness itself? My selfishness is unsurpassed. I know not what it means to love. I have not learned the first step. I have nothing to love with. I feel bereft of love, of the capacity to love. I am in a boat tossed to and fro by thoughts, imaginations, and helplessness!

Oh, God, I give You the only thing I possess—my wretchedness. I give You my weaknesses. I give You my selfishness. I give You my infidelities. I give You my sins. I give You my nothingness, my abject poverty of soul. I place my small unfaithful soul, that is incapable of any good, into Your Hands. I place my selfish love into the wound in Your Heart. I place my wandering, aimless mind under Your thorn-crowned Head. I wait for Your Mercy to envelop me. Your Hand to reach down to forgive me—Your Heart to flood my soul with new strength. I wait. I cannot complain because You delay. I am not worthy that You should take a thought of me, but I wait, hoping for Your Mercy to teach me how to love. I cannot do it on my own. I wait, how long, oh Lord? Where is Your Light? I stand still, afraid to move forward. I am alone. So alone.

OCTOBER 23, 1984

I thank Thee, oh Lord, for showing me the depths of my misery. How else can I know and understand Your Love and Mercy? How can You use me if I do not plumb the depths of my utter helplessness? I cry out to You, oh God, to teach me, show me my misery, but do not permit me to offend Thee. Lift this nothingness into Your Omnipotence and penetrate me through and through. Be gentle, Lord Jesus, as I lie prostrate before You waiting for Your Power to lift me up.

At Day's End

A Prayer in the Quiet of Night

In the quiet of the night, O God, I hear Your Silent Presence. The night brings on a deep silence and it is as if creation stands still while Your Presence gives all creatures strength for another day. Heal my soul during this night, dear Lord, and let Your Compassion and Mercy penetrate my being so tomorrow may be a day of new beginnings. Pour the love of the Holy Spirit into my heart that I may pattern my life after Jesus. Amen.

A Final Thanks

Thank You, Jesus, for the graces and gifts of this day. I praise You for the sorrow that detached me and the joy that made me so aware of Your Presence. I love You, Lord God. Make me like You.

A PRAYER AT DAY'S END

Good night, Lord. Thank You for Your Grace and Strength today. I didn't do all the things I wanted to. I wasn't like Jesus all the times I could have been and I didn't think of You as much as my soul needed to. All in all, it wasn't the day I planned when I saw the light this morning. I have acquired more self-knowledge and I do realize I need to put forth more effort. I am the recipient of Your Merciful Love for once again You put up with my many frailties. It seems the only thing I have left tonight is my desire to know You better and love You more. I end the day a little more humbled by the realization of my weakness but exulting in Your Holiness and Goodness. I shall find my joy in You and not in myself. If I have grown in seeking You alone then it has been a good day indeed. Good night, dear Lord; let Your Angels protect me and intercede for me while I sleep. Let Your Son's Mother make ready many graces for tomorrow, that I may love You more and be more like Jesus. Amen.

The

PERSONAL DEVOTIONS

Perhaps no one in modern history has done more to prop-agate spiritual devotions than Mother Angelica. Via the airwaves and through her personal witness, she intro-duced millions to devotions long forgotten. What follows are those she practiced and encouraged.

Morning and Evening Prayers

ON AWAKENING AND ARISING IN THE MORNING

In Nomine Patris, et Filii, et Spiritus Sancti. Amen.

O Jesus, O Mary, to you I give my soul and my body as a morning holocaust. Most Holy Trinity, Triune God, I adore Thee and out of love for Thee I offer myself as servant of the Most Holy Sacrament. O Jesus in the Most Blessed Sacrament, my Love, grant that today I may serve Thee more faithfully and love Thee more ardently than I did yesterday, and that, hidden with Thee, I may be a true victim of love.

MORNING PRAYER

In Nomine Patris, et Filii, et Spiritus Sancti. Amen.

O Jesus, Thou Source of Life, in Whom all things exist, permit that at the beginning of this day I make a holy covenant with Thee and never separate myself from Thee. Inebriate my soul with the living stream of Thy Grace, that it may wash away every taint of sin and replenish it with supernatural life. Give me Thy Blessing, so that I may begin this day well, and employ and end it according to Thy Holy Will. Almighty Father, Whose Wisdom and Goodness are without number, annihilated before Thy Divine Majesty I adore Thee with profound humility, confessing my weakness and my baseness. I give Thee thanks for all the graces Thou hast lavished on me from the first moment of my life to the present hour; especially for having protected me during the past night and granted me this new day in order that I may consecrate it with love and fidelity entirely to Thy Holy Service. Oh most merciful Lord, support me with Thy Grace, so that by the faithful discharge of my duties I may deserve to be numbered among Thy servants and elect.

THE MORNING OFFERING

O my Jesus, prostrate before Thee I lay my poor soul at the feet of Thy Divine Majesty. Turn Thy eyes upon me, that I may know the true condition of my soul, the greatness of Thy Mercy and my ingratitude toward Thee. O Jesus hidden in the Most Holy Sacrament, King of my heart, I dare not raise my eyes to Thee, but I implore Thee for a look of mercy. In the name of our Sisters and united with them in holy love, I offer Thee this present day to *adore* Thee; to *thank* Thee for Thy Innumerable Graces, especially for having called us to the perpetual adoration of the Most Blessed Sacrament; to repair the infidelities and sins through which Thy Divine Heart is saddened by us; to implore at Thy Throne of Mercy the grace of perfect contrition, renewal of holy zeal, and a continual increase of Thy Most Pure Love.

This intention I offer Thee, O Jesus, through the Immaculate Heart of Thy beloved Mother, in union with all that Thy Eucharistic Heart here fulfills toward the eternal Father. O my sweetest Jesus, bless me, Thy poorest servant, and grant me the grace to pass this day at Thy feet. Oh, may I not lose a moment of it, but offer each one according to Thy good pleasure!

Most blessed and Immaculate Mother of Jesus, I place myself entirely under thy protection. Instruct, enlighten, and direct me; support me in my weakness; and adore our dear Lord for me, since thou art my only refuge. St. Joseph, holy Father Francis, holy Mother Clare, my Guardian Angel and my Patron saints, pray for me and obtain the grace that this may be for me a day of true conversion. May it be so spent as if it were my last here on earth, thus serving as preparation for a blessed eternity, for which my soul longs, in order forever to adore, love, and possess my God. Amen.

EVENING ACT OF REPARATION

Eternal Father, I offer Thee the Sacred Heart of Jesus, with all His Love, His Sufferings, and His Merits:

1. In atonement for all the sins and imperfections I have committed this day and during my whole life.

Glory be to the Father and to the Son, and to the Holy Spirit as it was in the beginning, is now, and ever shall be. Amen.

2. To purify all the good I have done badly this day and during my whole life. Glory be . . .

3. To supply for all the good I should have done and neglected to do today and during my whole life.

Glory be . . . (PCPA Prayer Book)

EVENING COVENANT

My God, if I am to die tomorrow or suddenly at any time, I wish to receive Holy Communion in the morning as my Viaticum. I desire that my last food may be the Body and Blood of my Savior and Redeemer; my last words: Jesus, Mary, Joseph; my last affection an act of pure love of God and of perfect contrition for my sins; my last consolation to die in Thy Holy Love and in Thy Holy Grace. Amen.

Divine Providence

LITANY OF DIVINE PROVIDENCE

Mother Angelica's reliance on Divine Providence in her personal and professional life is legendary. This classic doctrine has been described by Dominican theologian Fr. Reginald Garrigou-Lagrange as "God's loving care for man and the need for confidence in Almighty God." Here from the PCPA Prayer Book is the litany Mother prayed for greater faith in Divine Providence.

Lord, have mercy on us   *Christ, have mercy on us*
Lord, have mercy on us
Christ, hear us   *Christ, graciously hear us*
God, the Father of heaven   *Have mercy on us (continue)*
God, the Son, Redeemer of the world
God, the Holy Ghost

Holy Trinity, one God

Divine Providence, glance of love

Divine Providence, Who dost govern us and provide for us
with paternal care

Divine Providence, hope of our salvation

Divine Providence, consolation of the poor pilgrim soul

Divine Providence, our protection in danger

Divine Providence, giver of all gifts

Divine Providence, treasury of gifts and graces without number

Divine Providence, support of the just

Divine Providence, hope of sinners and of the forsaken

Divine Providence, refuge of the exiled

Divine Providence, peace of our hearts

Divine Providence, consoler of the sorrowful

Divine Providence, refreshment of the thirsty

Divine Providence, efficacious remedy for all evils

Divine Providence, giver of all consolation

Divine Providence, protector of the poor

Divine Providence, support of widows and of orphans

Divine Providence, divine attribute, worthy of all our
veneration, confidence, and love

Lamb of God, Who takest away the sins of the world

Spare us, O Lord

Lamb of God, Who takest away the sins of the world

Graciously hear us, O Lord

Lamb of God, Who takest away the sins of the world

Have mercy on us

Christ, hear us   *Christ, graciously hear us*

Let us pray.

O God, Whose Providence cannot err in its ordinances, we humbly implore Thee to remove everything hurtful, and to grant us what is beneficial. Through our Lord Jesus Christ. Amen.

FINDING THE TRUE PRESENCE

Today you have a hard time finding Jesus. But if you can find that lit lamp in the church, then you know where the Lord is. That light indicates that in that tabernacle is the Love of All Love—Infinite Love. You can't love unless you get close to love. You can't have a fire unless you get close to a fire. You can't be warm unless you're near the heat. We have to know that we are loved by a God who is real and present.

—*Mother Angelica*

The Blessed Sacrament

ACT OF ADORATION OF JESUS IN THE MOST BLESSED SACRAMENT

If Mother Angelica spent her life practicing one devotion more than any other, it was adoration of Christ in the Blessed Sacrament. For Mother and her nuns it is the very center of their lives. They have vowed to worship Jesus Christ in the Blessed Sacrament and offer reparation for mankind.

They dedicate hours each day fulfilling this obligation. This prayer comes from the Poor Clares of Perpetual Adoration Prayer Book and was in use at the time Mother Angelica entered the order. Not only did she pray this prayer during her personal hours of Eucharistic adoration, but as a young sister, she sent signed copies of it to friends and supporters.

I adore Thee, O Jesus, God of Love, truly present in the Most Holy Sacrament. I adore Thee Who hast come to Thy Own, but was not received by them. I adore Thee Whom the majority of mankind reject and despise. I adore Thee Whom the impious incessantly offend by their sacrileges and blasphemies. I adore Thee Who art grieved by the coldness and indifference even of a vast number of Christians. I adore Thee, O Infinite Goodness, Who hast wrought so many miracles, in order to reveal Thy love to us. I adore Thee with all the angels and saints, and with these chosen souls that are now already the blessed of Thy Father, and are all aglow with burning love to Thee. I adore Thee with all Thy friends, O Jesus! With them I prostrate myself at the foot of the altar, to offer Thee my most profound homage, to receive Thy Divine Inspiration, and to implore Thy Grace. Oh, how good it is for me to be here with Thee! How sweet to hear the voice of my Beloved! Oh Victim of Divine Love! A piercing cry breaks forth from Thy Heart here on the altar, as once it did on Calvary; it is the cry of Love. "I thirst," Thou callest to Thy children, "I thirst for your love! Come all you whom I love as my Father has loved me; come and quench the thirst that consumes me!"

Lord Jesus, behold, I come! My heart is small, but it is

all Thy Own. Thou art a prisoner in our tabernacles, Thou, the Lord of lords! And love it is that holds Thee here as such! Thou leavest the tabernacle only to come to us, to unite Thyself with the faithful soul, and allow Thy Divine Love to reign in her. O King of Love, come, live, reign in me! I want no other law but the law of Thy Love. No, no, I henceforth desire to know naught, neither of the world, nor of what is in it, nor of myself; Thy Love alone shall rule in me eternally! O Jesus, grant me this grace. Break all my fetters, strip me of all that is not Thyself, in order that Thy Love may be my life here below, and my happiness and delight in eternity. Amen.

Offering of the Precious Blood

Eternal Father, I offer Thee the most Precious Blood of our Lord Jesus, in union with the Immaculate Virgin Mary and in her name, and in union with all the saints in heaven and the elect on earth, in thanksgiving for all the gifts and privileges with which Thou hast adorned her as Thy most obedient Daughter, but especially for the gift of her Immaculate Conception. I offer Thee the Most Precious Blood also for the conversion of sinners, for the spread and exaltation of our holy Mother the Church, for the preservation and welfare of her visible Head, the sovereign Roman Pontiff and according to his intentions. Glory be . . .

Eternal Incarnate Word, I offer Thee Thy most Precious Blood in union with the Immaculate Virgin Mary and in her name, and in union with all the saints in heaven and the elect on earth, in thanksgiving for all the gifts and privileges with which Thou hast adorned her as Thy most beloved Mother, but especially for the gift of her Immaculate Conception.

I offer Thee Thy most Precious Blood also for the conversion of sinners, for the spread and exaltation of our holy Mother the Church, for the preservation and welfare of her visible Head, the sovereign Roman Pontiff and according to his intentions. Glory be . . .

Eternal Holy Ghost, I offer Thee the most Precious Blood of Jesus, in union with the Immaculate Virgin Mary and in her name, and in union with all the saints in heaven and the elect on earth, in thanksgiving for all the gifts and privileges with which Thou hast adorned her as Thy Dearest Spouse, but especially for the gift of her Immaculate Conception.

I offer Thee the most Precious Blood also for the conversion of sinners, for the spread and exaltation of our holy Mother the Church, for the preservation and welfare of her visible Head, the sovereign Roman Pontiff and according to his intentions. Glory be . . .

OFFERING OF THE ADORATION HOUR

O sweetest Jesus, I thank Thee that Thou permittest me to visit Thee. I believe that Thou art truly present in this Most Holy Sacrament. I place all my trust in Thee, and I love Thee above all things. In union with all elect souls that have consecrated themselves exclusively to this Sacrament of Love here on earth, in union with all the angels and saints in heaven, with the Immaculate Heart of Thy most holy Mother, and with Thy own Divine Eucharistic Heart, O Jesus, I offer Thee this hour of adoration to praise Thee in this Sacrament of Love; to thank Thee for all gifts and graces, especially for this adorable Sacrament; to offer reparation to Thy Divine Heart for all the abuses and ingratitude that Thou must endure in this Sacrament; and to implore Thy mercy for all necessary graces . . . especially that Thou mayest be better known and more loved in this dearest Sacrament of Thy Heart. O Lord, grant me the grace to spend this precious hour in such a manner as not to lose one moment of it, and to obtain Thy mercy. Amen.

EUCHARISTIC CONSECRATION

I offer myself entirely to Thy Eucharistic Heart, through the Immaculate Heart of Thy Mother, and I implore Thee to preserve me as Thy property from every sin, and to give me grace and strength to overcome every temptation. Grant especially, O dearest Jesus, whatever is necessary for me to be a true and faithful servant of the Most Blessed Sacrament. I petition these graces also, O dearest Lord, for all my dear brothers and sisters in faith.

PRAYER AT THE CLOSE OF THE ADORATION HOUR

Why must I leave Thee so soon, my sweetest Jesus? Why can I not while away all the hours of my life at Thy blessed feet? I thank Thee most sincerely and most humbly for having endured me in Thy Holy Presence. I thank Thee for all the graces that Thou hast granted to me and to others in this hour. Forgive me, my dearest Jesus, all the ingratitude and tepidity with which I have grieved Thy Most Loving Heart. Grant me all my petitions, so that my heart may not depart from Thee for one moment, but may with Thy Immaculate Mother, love Thee ever more and more in this Most Holy Sacrament. Give Thy Spirit to me, the poorest and the weakest of Thy servants, O Lord. Bless me, and may this blessing always remain with me.

In the Name of the Father, and of the Son, and of the Holy Ghost. Amen.

The Sacred Heart

DEVOTION TO THE SACRED HEART

Mother Angelica was a great advocate of the Sacred Heart. She told her nuns during one of their lessons: "St. Margaret Mary said, 'I saw His Divine Heart more brilliant than the sun transparent. This Heart and its adorable wound was encircled by a crown of thorns which signified the pricks our sins cause it. It was surrounded by a cross that signified the first moment of His Incarnation. When the Sacred Heart was formed, the cross was placed in His Heart. Our Lord made me understand the ardent desire He has to be loved by mankind!' See, that's what boggles my mind. He wants to be loved by you. St. Margaret Mary continues: 'So many go by the path of perdition and run in great numbers away from Him.' You know, it's very difficult for you and I to realize that God Who is Love Himself, Who is totally independent and totally self-sufficient and doesn't need anyone—desires and wills to need me and need you. I think if we knew that our whole lives would change."

Act of Consecration of the Community to the Sacred Heart

O Sacred Heart of Jesus, who revealed to St. Margaret Mary your ardent desire to reign over the whole world, behold us assembled here today to proclaim Your absolute dominion over our Community.

Henceforth we desire to live with Your Life so that among us may flourish the virtues for which You promised peace on earth, and for this end we will banish from our midst the spirit of the world which You abhor so much. You will reign over our understanding by the simplicity of our faith. You will reign over our hearts by an ardent love for You; and may the flame of this love be ever kept burning in our hearts by the fervent offering of Mass and devout reception of the Holy Eucharist. Be pleased, O Divine Heart, to preside over our meetings, to bless our undertakings both spiritual and temporal, to banish all worry and care, to sanctify our joys and soothe our sorrows. If any of us should ever have the misfortune to grieve Your Sacred Heart, remind her of Your Goodness and Mercy toward the repentant sinner.

And when the hour of separation strikes and death enters our community, whether we go or whether we stay, we shall all bow humbly before Your eternal decrees. This shall be our consolation—to remember that the day will come when our entire community, once more united in heaven, shall be able to sing of Your Glory and Your Goodness forever. May the Immaculate Heart of Mary and the glorious Patriarch St. Joseph vouchsafe to offer You our Act of Consecration, and to keep the memory thereof alive in us all the days of our lives. Glory to the Heart of Jesus, our King and our Father!

First Friday Renewal of Our Consecration

Mother Angelica on the First Friday Devotion: "The First Friday of every month Our Dear Lord asked that we go to Mass and Holy Communion. Let me tell you what Our Dear Lord promised St. Margaret Mary, if we fulfill His request. He said, 'I will give souls devoted to Me all the graces of their state in life.' He wants our love so badly! 'I will establish peace in their family.' Is that why there's no peace in our families, because we have not devoted ourselves to the love of Jesus? 'I will bless every house in which a picture of My Heart is exposed in honor. I will counsel them in their difficulties. I will be their refuge during life and at hour of death. I will pour abundant blessings upon their undertakings. Sinners shall find in My Heart a fountain of a boundless ocean of mercy. Tepid souls, lukewarm souls shall become fervent. Fervent souls shall rise speedily to great holiness. I will give to priests the power of touching the hardest hearts. Those who propagate this devotion shall have their names written in My Heart, never to be blotted out . . . and all those who receive Communion on the First Friday of the month for nine consecutive months will receive the grace of final penitence.' That means at the end of your life, you shall have total repentance. Oh boy! Can you imagine God loving you so much that He's going to make all these promises because He wants you to love Him? It just manifests to me that burning fire in the Heart of Jesus who calls all humanity to Himself."

Most kind Jesus, humbly kneeling at Your feet we renew our consecration to Your Divine Heart. Be our King Forever! In

You we have full and entire confidence. May Your Spirit penetrate our thoughts, our desires, our words, and our deeds. Bless our undertakings; share in our joys, in our trials, and in our daily labors. Grant us to know You better, to love You more, to serve You without faltering.

By the Immaculate Heart of Mary, Queen of Peace, set up Your kingdom in our country. Enter closely into the midst of our families and make them Your own through the solemn Enthronement of Your Sacred Heart, so that soon one cry may resound from home to home: "May the triumphant Heart of Jesus be everywhere loved, blessed, and glorified forever! Honor and glory to the Sacred Hearts of Jesus and Mary!" Most Sacred Heart of Jesus, Your kingdom come! Immaculate Heart of Mary, pray for us! St. Joseph, Friend of the Sacred Heart, pray for us!

Lord, have mercy on us.

Christ, have mercy on us.

Lord, have mercy on us.

Christ, hear us.

Christ, graciously hear us.

God, the Father of heaven, have mercy on us.

God the Son, Redeemer of the world,

God the Holy Spirit,

Holy Trinity, one God,

Heart of Jesus, Son of the eternal Father,

Heart of Jesus, formed by the Holy Spirit in the Virgin Mother's womb,

Heart of Jesus, substantially united to the Word of God,

Heart of Jesus, of infinite majesty,

Heart of Jesus, holy temple of God,

Heart of Jesus, tabernacle of the Most High,

Heart of Jesus, house of God and gate of heaven,

Heart of Jesus, glowing furnace of charity,

Heart of Jesus, vessel of justice and love,

Heart of Jesus, full of goodness and love,

Heart of Jesus, abyss of all virtues,

Heart of Jesus, most worthy of all praise,

Heart of Jesus, King and center of all hearts,

Heart of Jesus, wherein are all the treasures of wisdom and
knowledge,

Heart of Jesus, wherein dwells all the fullness of the Godhead,

Heart of Jesus, in whom the Father is well pleased,

Heart of Jesus, of whose fullness we have all received,

Heart of Jesus, desire of the everlasting hills,

Heart of Jesus, patient and rich in mercy,

Heart of Jesus, rich unto all who call upon You,

Heart of Jesus, fount of life and holiness,

Heart of Jesus, propitiation for our offenses,

Heart of Jesus, overwhelmed with reproaches,

Heart of Jesus, bruised for our iniquities,

Heart of Jesus, obedient even unto death,

Heart of Jesus, pierced with a lance,

Heart of Jesus, source of all consolation,

Heart of Jesus, our life and resurrection,

Heart of Jesus, our peace and reconciliation,

Heart of Jesus, victim for our sins,

Heart of Jesus, salvation of those who hope in You,

Heart of Jesus, hope of those who die in You,

Heart of Jesus, delight of all saints,

Lamb of God, who takes away the sins of the world, spare us,
O Lord.

Lamb of God, who takes away the sins of the world, graciously
hear us, O Lord.

Lamb of God, who takes away the sins of the world, have
mercy on us.

V. Jesus, meek and humble of heart,

R. Make our hearts like unto Yours.

Let us pray.

Almighty everlasting God, look upon the Heart of Your
dearly beloved Son, and upon the praise and satisfaction He offers
You in the name of sinners and for those who seek Your mercy. Be
appeased, and grant us pardon in the name of Jesus Christ, Your
Son, who lives and reigns with You forever and ever. Amen.

CONSECRATION TO THE SACRED HEART

O Sacred Heart of Jesus, filled with infinite love, broken by
my ingratitude, pierced by my sins, yet loving me still, accept
the consecration that I make to Thee of all that I am and all
that I have. Take every faculty of my soul and body, and draw
me day by day nearer and nearer to Thy sacred Side; and
there, as I can bear the lesson, teach me Thy blessed ways.
Amen.

Most Sacred Heart of Jesus, have mercy on us.

Most Sacred Heart of Jesus, have mercy on us.
Most Sacred Heart of Jesus, have mercy on us.

The Divine Child Jesus

DEVOTIONS TO THE CHILD JESUS

Mother Angelica's fervent devotion to the Child Jesus did not begin until the summer of 1996. It occurred during a trip to Bogota, Colombia. While visiting the Sanctuary of the Divino Niño, Mother claims a statue of the Child Jesus moved and spoke to her. He instructed her to build Him "a temple." Three years later she dedicated the Shrine of the Most Blessed Sacrament in Hanceville, Alabama, to the Divine Child. Of her attachment to the Child Jesus she said: "I want very much to spread devotion to the Divine Child Jesus. Not only is He powerful, but what you and I need is family—and that Child Jesus will make us one again. He will put love in our hearts, where it should be."

INSCRIPTION BEFORE THE DIVINO NIÑO STATUE, SHRINE OF THE MOST BLESSED SACRAMENT

The Divine Child Jesus is inviting us to accept His love, His heart and to carry with us and within us the Childhood of Jesus. May we all be led by the Divino Niño, Jesus.

—*Mother Angelica*

The Little King of Love

Divine Child Jesus who sheds your blessing on whoever invokes Your name, look kindly on us who kneel humbly before You and hear our prayers. We commend to Your Mercy the poor and needy people who trust in Your Divine Heart. Lay Your all-powerful hand upon them and help them in their needs. Lay Your hand upon the sick, to cure them and sanctify their suffering; upon those in distress, to console them; upon sinners to draw them into Your Divine Grace; upon all those who, stricken with grief and suffering, turn trustingly to You for loving help. Lay your hand upon all of us and give us Your Blessing. Oh little King, grant the treasures of Your Divine Mercy to all the world, and keep us now and always in the grace of Your Love. Amen.

Litany of the Infant Jesus

Lord, have mercy on us   *Christ, have mercy on us*
Lord, have mercy on us
Christ, hear us   *Christ, graciously hear us*
God the Father of heaven   *Have mercy on us (continue)*
God the Son, Redeemer of the world
God the Holy Ghost
Holy Trinity, one God
Infant Jesus, Son of the living Cod
Infant Jesus, Son of the Virgin Mary

Infant Jesus, begotten before the morning star

Infant Jesus, Word made flesh

Infant Jesus, wisdom of the Father

Infant Jesus, purity of Thy Holy Mother

Infant Jesus, only-begotten Son of the Father

Infant Jesus, only-born of Thy Mother

Infant Jesus, image of the Father

Infant Jesus, Creator of Thy Mother

Infant Jesus, splendor of the Father

Infant Jesus, honor of Thy Mother

Infant Jesus, equal to the Father

Infant Jesus, subject to Thy Mother

Infant Jesus, joy of Thy Father

Infant Jesus, riches of Thy Mother

Infant Jesus, gift of Thy Father

Infant Jesus, gift of Thy Mother

Infant Jesus, precious fruit of a Virgin

Infant Jesus, Creator of man

Infant Jesus, our God

Infant Jesus, our Brother

Infant Jesus, perfect man from Thy conception

Infant Jesus, Father of ages

Infant Jesus, eternal Word, making Thyself dumb

Infant Jesus, weeping in Thy crib

Infant Jesus, joy of paradise

Infant Jesus, exiled from Thy people

Infant Jesus, strong in weakness

Infant Jesus, powerful in abasement

Infant Jesus, treasure of grace

Infant Jesus, fountain of love

Infant Jesus, Author of the blessings of heaven

Infant Jesus, repairer of the evils of earth

Infant Jesus, head of angels

Infant Jesus, expectation of nations

Infant Jesus, joy of the shepherds

Infant Jesus, light of the Magi

Infant Jesus, salvation of children

Infant Jesus, hope of the just

Infant Jesus, teacher of doctors

Be merciful   *Spare us, O Infant Jesus*

Be merciful   *Graciously hear us, O Infant Jesus*

From the bondage of the children of Adam

Deliver us, O Infant Jesus

(continue)

From the slavery of the devil

From the corruption of the world

From the lust of the flesh

From the pride of life

From blindness of mind

From perversity of will

From our sins

Through Thy pure conception

Through Thy humble birth

Through Thy tears

Through Thy painful circumcision

Through Thy glorious epiphany

Through Thy devout presentation

Through Thy most holy life

Through Thy poverty

Through Thy sorrows

Through Thy obedience

Through Thy labors and trials

Lamb of God, Who takest away the sins of the world

Spare us, O Infant Jesus

Lamb of God, Who takest away the sins of the world

Graciously hear us, O Infant Jesus

Lamb of God, Who takest away the sins of the world

Have mercy on us, O Infant Jesus

Infant Jesus, hear us   *Infant Jesus, graciously hear us*

Let us pray.

O Lord Jesus Christ, Who didst vouchsafe so to annihilate the greatness of Thy Incarnate Divinity and most sacred humanity, as to be born in time and become a little child; grant that we may acknowledge infinite wisdom in the silence of a child, power in weakness, majesty in abasement; so that adoring Thy Humiliations on earth, we may contemplate Thy Glories in heaven, Who with the Father and the Holy Ghost livest and reignest, God, forever and ever. Amen. (PCPA Prayer Book)

PRAYER TO THE CHILD JESUS

O miraculous Child Jesus! I come before Your Sacred Image, moved by love and by hope, and I beseech You to look mercifully into my troubled heart. Let Your own tender Love, always inclined to compassion, mitigate my troubles and alleviate my sufferings. Take from me, if it be Your Will, all unbearable afflictions and let me never surrender to despair. Grant me, Dear Child Jesus, the special grace I ask from You today in all humility and with a loving trust, and for the sake of Your Sacred Infancy, always hear my prayers. Be generous with your aid and consolation, that I may praise You, and the Father, and the Holy Spirit. Amen.

A PRAYER OF THANKSGIVING TO THE DIVINE CHILD JESUS

Most gracious Infant Jesus, in humble adoration I offer You most fervent thanks for all the blessings You have bestowed upon me. I shall always praise Your ineffable Mercy and confess that You alone are my God, my Helper, and my Protector.

Henceforth, my entire confidence shall be placed in You. Everywhere will I proclaim Your Mercy and Generosity, so that Your great Love and the great Deeds which You perform may be acknowledged by all. May devotion to Your Most Holy Infancy extend more and more in the hearts of all Christians and may all who experience Your Assistance persevere in returning unceasing gratitude to Your Most Holy Infancy to which be praise and glory for all eternity. Amen.

Divine Child Jesus, bless and protect us. Amen.

Everything you want to ask, do it through the merits of My Infancy and your prayers will be heard.

—*Jesus to Ven. Margaret of the Most Holy Sacrament*

EVENING HYMN TO THE DIVINE CHILD

My Jesus dear, my heart's delight.
We come to say '"Good Night!"
Our wrongs, our faults, our misdeeds all,
Our hearts sincere regret.
And for all graces we received
A thousand thanks, as 'tis but meet;
Thy Infant feet, O let us kiss,
O Jesus dear, sweet Jesus.

Oh, would that we could linger e'er
At Thy dear feet, sweet Jesus,
And rest before Thy lonely shrine
Where Thou art mine, all mine.
O rapture sweet, at Jesus' feet
I place my heart the while I sleep,
That here sweet vigil it may keep.
With Jesus dear, sweet Jesus.

And thus my slumbering heart shall wake
E'en though my eyelids close;
And Thy bless'd Mother's watchful heart
Pour forth its love o'er mine.
My heart alone for Thee shall beat.
My soul bear 'lone Thy image sweet;
In slumber as in wakeful hours,
This heart Thee'll love, sweet Jesus! (PCPA Prayer Book)

The Saints

PRAYER TO ST. JOSEPH

O St. Joseph, whose protection is so great, so strong, so prompt before the Throne of God, I place in you all my interests and desires. O St. Joseph, do assist me by your powerful intercession and obtain for me from your Divine Son all spiritual blessings through Jesus Christ, Our Lord; so that having engaged here below your Heavenly power, I may offer my thanksgiving and homage to the most loving of Fathers. O St. Joseph, I never weary of contemplating you and Jesus asleep in your arms. I dare not approach while He reposes near your heart. Press Him in my name and kiss His fine Head for me, and ask Him to return the kiss when I draw my dying breath. St. Joseph, Patron of departing souls, pray for us. Amen.

NOVENA TO ST. THERESE

Rita Rizzo (Mother Angelica) suffered from a lingering stomach malady during her youth. In January 1943, a mystic named Rhoda Wise gave the twenty-one-year-old Rita the following prayer. The woman told her to recite it for nine days and to beg St. Therese's prayers for a healing. (The full story is in Mother Angelica: The Remarkable Story of a Nun, Her Nerve, and a Network of Miracles. *At the conclusion of the nine days Rita Rizzo was healed of her stomach troubles and a great love affair with God began. Here is the much requested prayer in its original form.*

Oh beautiful Rose of Carmel, St. Therese of the Infant Jesus, deign according to your promise to descend from heaven to visit those who implore you. Pour down on us in profusion those celestial graces that are symbolized by the shower of roses that Jesus your Spouse has put in your disposition. Your power is great with His Heart. He can only listen and hear your prayer. I have then recourse to you.

Oh St. Therese of the Infant Jesus, assist me in this circumstance. Speak for me to Jesus and to Mary to obtain for me to live a holy life and die a happy death. Amen.

St. Therese hear my prayer. Show your power with God and cure me if it be for the honor of God, and the good of my soul. Amen.

In Honor of St. Francis

Heaven's splendor shown, a new celestial figure became visible to Holy Father Francis most brilliant, to whom the seraph appeared, imprinting a wound in his palms, soles, and side. Therefore, the likeness of the Cross strove he to manifest by his heart, mouth, and labor.

V. Thou hast signed, O Lord, Thy servant Francis.

R. With the sign of Redemption.

Let us pray.

Lord Jesus Christ, Who when the world was growing cold, to inflame our hearts with the fire of Thy love, didst renew the prints of Thy Sacred Passion in the body of most Blessed Francis, graciously grant that by his merits and prayers, we may always carry our cross, and bring forth worthy fruits of penance. (PCPA Prayer Book)

In Honor of St. Anthony

If thou seekest miracles —
Death, error, all calamities
The leprosy and demons fly
The sick, by him made whole, arise.
The sea withdraws and fetters break
And withered limbs he doth restore
While treasures lost are found again,
When young or old his help implore.

All dangers vanish from our path
Our direst needs do quickly flee;
Let those who know repeat the theme:
Let Paduans praise St. Anthony.
V. Pray for us, O Blessed Anthony.
R. That we may be made worthy of the promises of Christ.

Let us pray.

Let Thy Church, O God, be gladdened by the solemn commemoration of blessed Anthony, Thy Confessor: that she may evermore be defended by Thy spiritual assistance, and merit to possess everlasting joy. (PCPA Prayer Book)

The Angels

PRAYERS TO THE ANGELS

These two prayers, composed by Mother Angelica, reveal her devotion to God's Messengers of Light. Since her encounter with an angel as a young girl, when she felt two hands lift her out of the path of an oncoming bus, Mother Angelica was always a fierce promoter of the angels and spread devotion to them whenever she could.

St. Michael and all you holy Angels, protect us from the snares of the evil spirits. Instill into our minds thoughts of repentance and love and obtain for us from the Throne of the Most High the Gifts of the Spirit and a bright reflection of Jesus in our souls. Amen.

Angels of God, bright creatures of His Infinite Power, I am humbled at the thought of Your love and concern for me. When I think that you are my brothers in the Lord, mighty protectors against the malice of the Enemy, I feel a surge of courage fill my soul. Tell me, Angelic Spirits, how can I best please the Most High? You who have never offended Our Lord and God, have pity on my poor, weak human nature and inspire me with those thoughts and deeds that will please our Father in Heaven. Warn me of dangers and guide me in the paths of holiness. Help me avoid occasions of sin and give me light to see God's plan in my life. Intercede for me before the Throne of God and tell Him I love Him. Amen.

THE ANGEL'S PRAYER AT FATIMA

Mother and her community pray the following each day:

My God, I believe, I adore, I hope, and I love You. I ask forgiveness for all those who do not believe, do not adore, do not hope, and do not love You.

Most Holy Trinity, Father, Son, and Holy Spirit, I adore You profoundly, and I offer You the Most Precious Body, Blood, Soul, and Divinity of Jesus Christ, present in all the tabernacles of the world, in reparation for the outrages, sacrileges, and indifferences by which He is offended, and by the infinite merits of His Most Sacred Heart, and through the Immaculate Heart of Mary, I beg the conversion of poor sinners.

ST. RAPHAEL AND THE POWER OF THE ANGELS

October 24 (September 29 in the new Roman Calendar) is the Feast of St. Raphael. His name means "Medicine of God," and if ever the world needed a spiritual physician it needs it now. We are not fighting against politics, but against the forces of Satan: men who have given themselves over to the possession of the devil. Only God can help us. This is His battle. Remember that one Angel could wipe out a continent in no time at all. Let's remember how powerful the Angels are and ask them to help us.

—*Mother Angelica*

THE GUARDIAN ANGEL'S PRAYER

Angel of God, my guardian dear, to whom God's Love commits me here, ever this day, be at my side, to light, to guard, to rule, to guide. Amen.

THE CHAPLET OF ST. MICHAEL

It was not until after her stroke, in 2001, that Mother began reciting the Chaplet of St. Michael at the urging of fellow sisters in her community. In one of her final recorded devotions, Mother Angelica led the Chaplet, which at this writing is aired each morning on EWTN. The Chaplet was the work of Antonia d'Astonac, a Servant of God who claimed St. Michael told her to honor him by saluting each Choir of Angels. One Our Father and three Hail Marys are prayed after each "salutation." For those who pray the Chaplet each day, St. Michael promised that an angel from each of the choirs would accompany them to communion and that he would provide assistance throughout their lives. At death, he promised to deliver the devotee and their relatives from the pains of Purgatory. The devotion is prayed on a colorful chaplet. The colors are referenced below.

Begin the Chaplet by praying the following invocation on the medal:

V. O God, come to my aid.

R. O Lord, make haste to help me.

V. Glory be to the Father, and to the Son, and to the Holy Spirit.

R. As it was in the beginning, is now, and ever shall be, world without end. Amen.

The First Salutation (Ruby)

Through the intercession of St. Michael and the Celestial Choir of SERAPHIM, may it please God to make us worthy to receive into our hearts the Fire of His perfect Charity. Amen.

One Our Father, three Hail Marys.

The Second Salutation (Sapphire)

Through the intercession of St. Michael and the Celestial Choir of CHERUBIM, may God grant us the Grace to abandon the ways of sin and follow the path of Christian Perfection. Amen.

One Our Father, three Hail Marys.

The Third Salutation (Amethyst)

Through the intercession of St. Michael and the Celestial Choir of THRONES, may it please God to infuse into our hearts a true and earnest spirit of Humility. Amen.

One Our Father, three Hail Marys.

The Fourth Salutation (Crystal)

Through the intercession of St. Michael and the Celestial Choir of DOMINATIONS, may it please God to grant us the Grace to have dominion over our senses, and to correct our depraved passions. Amen.

One Our Father, three Hail Marys.

The Fifth Salutation (Garnet)

Through the intercession of St. Michael and the Celestial Choir of VIRTUES, may Our Lord keep us from falling into temptation and deliver us from evil. Amen.

One Our Father, three Hail Marys.

The Sixth Salutation (Aquamarine)

Through the intercession of St. Michael and the Celestial Choir of POWERS, may God vouchsafe to keep our souls from the wiles and the temptations of the devil. Amen.

One Our Father, three Hail Marys.

The Seventh Salutation (Emerald)

Through the intercession of St. Michael and the Celestial Choir of PRINCIPALITIES, may it please God to fill our hearts with the spirit of true and hearty Obedience. Amen

One Our Father, three Hail Marys.

The Eighth Salutation (Aurora Borealis)

Through the intercession of St. Michael and the Celestial Choir of ARCHANGELS, may it please God to grant us the Grace of Perseverance in the Faith and in all good works, that we may thereby be enabled to attain unto the glory of Paradise. Amen.

One Our Father, three Hail Marys.

The Ninth Salutation (Topaz)

Through the intercession of St. Michael and the Celestial Choir of ANGELS, may God vouchsafe to grant that they may protect us during life, and after death may lead us into the everlasting glory of Heaven. Amen.

One Our Father, three Hail Marys.

Then pray the Our Father four times in conclusion on the appropriate beads: the first in honor of ST. MICHAEL (Ruby), the second in honor of ST. GABRIEL (Sapphire), the third in honor of ST. RAPHAEL (Emerald), and the fourth in honor of your own GUARDIAN ANGEL (Topaz).

Conclude with the following:

St. Michael, glorious Prince, chief and champion of the Heavenly Hosts, guardian of the souls of men, conqueror of the rebellious angels, steward of the Palace of God under Our Divine King Jesus Christ; our worthy leader, endowed with super-human excellence and virtue: vouchsafe to free us from all evil, who with full confidence have recourse to thee; and by thy incomparable protection, enable us to make progress every day in the faithful service of Our God. Amen.

V. Pray for us, most blessed Michael, Prince of the Church of Jesus Christ.

R. That we may be made worthy of His promises.

Let us pray.

Almighty and Eternal God, Who in Thine Own marvelous goodness and pity, didst, for the common salvation of men, choose Thy glorious Archangel Michael, to be the Prince of Thy Church: make us worthy, we pray Thee, to be delivered by his beneficent protection from all our enemies, that, at the hour of our death, none of them may approach to harm us; rather do Thou vouchsafe unto us that, by the same Archangel Michael, we may be introduced into the Presence of Thy Most High and Divine Majesty. Through the Merits of the same Jesus Christ Our Lord. Amen.

> Prayer is, beyond doubt, the most powerful weapon the Lord gives us to conquer evil passions and temptations of the devil; but we must really put ourselves into our prayer: it is not enough just to say the words, it must come from the heart. And also prayer needs to be continuous, we must pray no matter what kind of situation we find ourselves in: the warfare we are engaged in is ongoing, so our prayer must be on-going also.
>
> —*St. Alphonsus de Liguori*

The Litany of Humility

O Jesus meek and humble of Heart, have mercy on me.
From the desire to be esteemed   *Deliver me, O Jesus*
From the desire to be loved
From the desire to be sought
From the desire to be honored
From the desire to be praised
From the desire to be preferred to others
From the desire to be asked for advice
From the desire to be approved
From the desire to be considered

From the fear to be humbled

From the fear to be despised

From the fear to be rebuffed

From the fear to be calumniated

From the fear to be forgotten

From the fear to be ridiculed

From the fear to be treated unfairly

From the fear to be suspected

That others be loved more than I   *O Jesus, grant me the grace*
to desire it

That others may be esteemed more than I

That others grow in the opinion of the world and I diminish

That others be entrusted with work and I be put aside

That others be praised and I neglected

That others be preferred before me in everything

That others be more holy than I, provided I am as holy as I
can be

The Stations of the Cross / Way of the Cross

THE STATIONS OF THE CROSS

From the first centuries Christians have observed the Way of the Cross,
meditating on Christ's path to Calvary. St. Jerome writes of pilgrims in

the early fifth century visiting the Holy Land and praying at the sites associated with the Lord's sufferings. When the Franciscans became custodians of the Holy Sites in 1342, the devotion continued to develop and spread throughout the world. Following that Franciscan tradition, Mother Angelica would lead her sisters in the Stations of the Cross each Friday during Lent. She offered them her own inspired meditations for each movement of the Passion. Since her time with Rhoda Wise, a mystic in Canton, Ohio, who bled from her hands and head during the Fridays of Lent, Mother Angelica had developed a deep personal attachment to the Passion of Christ. She would often weep as she offered these prayers to her nuns. Below are two versions of the Stations of the Cross, composed and recited by Mother Angelica for her community.

The First Station: Jesus Is Condemned to Death

In the name of the Father and of the Son and of the Holy Ghost, Amen.

We adore Thee, O Christ and we bless Thee.

R: Because by Your Holy Cross, You have redeemed the world.

Lord Jesus as you stand before Pilate, condemned so unjustly, may all those who are so misused, abused, and condemned unjustly have the courage to carry their cross. Lord, help all Christians to stand tall. And may you guide all sinners to You.

R: Hail Mary, full of Grace, the Lord is with thee, blessed art thou amongst women and blessed is the fruit of thy womb, Jesus. Holy Mary, Mother of God, pray for us sinners now and at the hour of our death. Amen. Most Sorrowful Mother, Pray for us.

The Second Station: Jesus Carries His Cross

We adore Thee, O Christ and we bless Thee.

R: Because by Your Holy Cross, You have redeemed the world.

Lord Jesus as You carry Your Cross, help all those who have a hard time carrying the cross. Help those that are sad and discouraged, disheartened, and confused with nowhere to go. Lord Jesus, help us to carry the burden that is our hopelessness, that we may do so with courage. Immaculate Heart of Mary, we consecrate all sinners to your heart.

R: Hail Mary, full of Grace, the Lord is with thee, blessed art thou amongst women and blessed is the fruit of thy womb, Jesus. Holy Mary, Mother of God, pray for us sinners now and at the hour of our death. Amen. Most Sorrowful Mother, Pray for us.

The Third Station: Jesus Falls the First Time

We adore Thee, O Christ and we bless Thee.

R: Because by Your Holy Cross, You have redeemed the world.

Lord Jesus as You fall the first time, we ask You to have mercy on all those who have moral weaknesses. After they fall over and over again, Lord, give them strength, courage, and grace to overcome their failings. Immaculate Heart of Mary, we give you all sinners.

R: Hail Mary, full of Grace, the Lord is with thee, blessed art thou amongst women and blessed is the fruit of thy womb, Jesus. Holy Mary, Mother of God, pray for us sinners now and at the hour of our death. Amen. Most Sorrowful Mother, Pray for us.

The Fourth Station: Jesus Meets His Afflicted Mother

We adore Thee, O Christ and we bless Thee.

R: Because by Your Holy Cross, You have redeemed the world.

Lord Jesus we thank You for comforting Your mother, and we thank Our Lady for comforting You. We ask You, Lord, to give Your Grace to all those who find it so painful to see their loved ones suffer and die. Give them courage. Immaculate Heart of Mary, pray for sinners.

R: Hail Mary, full of Grace, the Lord is with thee, blessed art thou amongst women and blessed is the fruit of thy womb, Jesus. Holy Mary, Mother of God, pray for us sinners now and at the hour of our death. Amen. Most Sorrowful Mother, Pray for us.

Fifth Station: Simon Helps Jesus Carry His Cross

We adore Thee, O Christ and we bless Thee.

R: Because by Your Holy Cross, You have redeemed the world.

Lord Jesus as Simon helped You to carry Your Cross, send other people, other sinners, to help those whose crosses are unbearable. Help them Lord to carry their cross. Send Thy angels, Lord, to help all people carry their cross amidst difficulties. Immaculate Heart of Mary we dedicate and consecrate all sinners to your heart.

R: Hail Mary, full of Grace, the Lord is with thee, blessed art thou amongst women and blessed is the fruit of thy womb, Jesus. Holy Mary, Mother of God, pray for us sinners now and at the hour of our death. Amen. Most Sorrowful Mother, Pray for us.

Sixth Station: Veronica Wipes the Face of Jesus

We adore Thee, O Christ and we bless Thee.

R: Because by Your Holy Cross, You have redeemed the world.

Lord Jesus, as Veronica wiped Your face, we ask that we may wipe Your face and comfort You during these terrible days in which we live. We ask, Lord, that You imprint Your image upon us, that we may radiate Your love and compassion. Immaculate Heart of Mary, we dedicate all souls to you.

R: Hail Mary, full of Grace, the Lord is with thee, blessed art thou amongst women and blessed is the fruit of thy womb, Jesus. Holy Mary, Mother of God, pray for us sinners now and at the hour of our death. Amen. Most Sorrowful Mother, Pray for us.

Seventh Station: Jesus Falls a Second Time

We adore Thee, O Christ and we bless Thee.

R: Because by Your Holy Cross, You have redeemed the world.

Jesus, as you fall the second time, have mercy on all abortionists, Lord, and all those who destroy human life. Give them light to change their ways. Through the power of Thy Spirit, Lord, change their hearts to see the evil they do. Immaculate Heart of Mary, we recommend and consecrate to you all those who may have ever had an abortion and those who may contemplate it today. May they have the grace embrace and defend life.

R: Hail Mary, full of Grace, the Lord is with thee, blessed art thou amongst women and blessed is the fruit of thy womb, Jesus.

Holy Mary, Mother of God, pray for us sinners now and at the hour of our death. Amen. Most Sorrowful Mother, Pray for us.

The Eighth Station: Jesus Speaks to the Holy Women

We adore Thee, O Christ and we bless Thee.
R: Because by Your Holy Cross, You have redeemed the world.
Lord Jesus, as you comfort the holy women, teach all of us to think of others and to comfort others—even though we ourselves may be in great pain or sorrow. Give us that grace of self-forgetfulness. Immaculate Heart of Mary, we dedicate and consecrate all sinners to you.
R: Hail Mary, full of Grace, the Lord is with thee, blessed art thou amongst women and blessed is the fruit of thy womb, Jesus. Holy Mary, Mother of God, pray for us sinners now and at the hour of our death. Amen. Most Sorrowful Mother, Pray for us.

The Ninth Station: Jesus Falls the Third Time

We adore Thee, O Christ and we bless Thee.
R: Because by Your Holy Cross, You have redeemed the world.
Lord Jesus, as You fall the third time, we offer this terrible pain for all the children of the world who are enslaved by addiction, alcohol, drugs, prostitution—all those lost in error. Lord, we ask Your Mercy upon them through the merits of this pain. Immaculate Heart of Mary, we consecrate to you all sinners and all children.
R: Hail Mary, full of Grace, the Lord is with thee, blessed art thou amongst women and blessed is the fruit of thy womb, Jesus. Holy Mary, Mother of God, pray for us sinners now

*and at the hour of our death. Amen. Most Sorrowful Mother,
Pray for us.*

The Tenth Station: Jesus Is Stripped of His Garments

We adore Thee, O Christ and we bless Thee.

R: Because by Your Holy Cross, You have redeemed the world.

Lord Jesus as You are stripped of Your garments, we offer
this terrible pain for all those who have moral problems,
Lord, for all the rich that are so attached to their goods.
For all of us, Lord, we have our own separate
attachments. We ask, Lord, through this terrible pain,
that You give us the grace to be detached. Most
Immaculate Heart of Mary, we consecrate all sinners
to you.

*R: Hail Mary, full of Grace, the Lord is with thee, blessed art thou
amongst women and blessed is the fruit of thy womb, Jesus.
Holy Mary, Mother of God, pray for us sinners now and at the
hour of our death. Amen. Most Sorrowful Mother, Pray for us.*

The Eleventh Station: Jesus Is Nailed to the Cross

We adore Thee, O Christ and we bless Thee.

R: Because by Your Holy Cross, You have redeemed the world.

Lord Jesus as You are nailed to the Cross, we ask You to
have mercy on all priests, all religious, bishops,
cardinals, our Holy Father. Grant that all priests and
religious may be faithful. Have mercy on those who
have strayed, those who are in error, those who preach
error. Have mercy on them all, that they may be brought

back to Your Heart and be a comfort to You.
Immaculate Heart of Mary, we consecrate all religious
and priests to your Immaculate Heart.

R: *Hail Mary, full of Grace, the Lord is with thee, blessed art thou amongst women and blessed is the fruit of thy womb, Jesus. Holy Mary, Mother of God, pray for us sinners now and at the hour of our death. Amen. Most Sorrowful Mother, Pray for us.*

The Twelfth Station: Jesus Dies on the Cross

We adore Thee, O Christ and we bless Thee.
R: *Because by Your Holy Cross, You have redeemed the world.*

Lord Jesus, we offer Your six hours of agony, Your death and all Your pain, for the whole world. Lord, have mercy upon us. We ask You, Lord, to come and save us. Help those in error. We offer this terrible pain for our work, Lord. Bless our labors and do wonders with it and let Your providence be manifest, that we may continue our work. Immaculate Heart of Mary, we consecrate the world to you, especially Russia.

R: *Hail Mary, full of Grace, the Lord is with thee, blessed art thou amongst women and blessed is the fruit of thy womb, Jesus. Holy Mary, Mother of God, pray for us sinners now and at the hour of our death. Amen. Most Sorrowful Mother, Pray for us.*

The Thirteenth Station: Jesus Is Taken Down from the Cross

We adore Thee, O Christ and we bless Thee.
R: *Because by Your Holy Cross, You have redeemed the world.*

Sweet Mother, as you take your Son down from the Cross and you see all the terrible wounds and agonies and all the pain He suffered, we ask that we may have some of your compassion for sinners and for our own weaknesses. Holy Mother, we consecrate all sinners to your Immaculate Heart.

R: *Hail Mary, full of Grace, the Lord is with thee, blessed art thou amongst women and blessed is the fruit of thy womb, Jesus. Holy Mary, Mother of God, pray for us sinners now and at the hour of our death. Amen. Most Sorrowful Mother, Pray for us.*

The Fourteenth Station: Jesus Is Laid in the Sepulcher

We adore Thee, O Christ and we bless Thee.

R: *Because by Your Holy Cross, You have redeemed the world.*

Sweet Mother, as you trusted so beautifully in God's providence to supply a tomb for your Son's body, obtain for us an increase of faith, that under the most trying circumstances, we may continue to believe in His Glory, His Divinity, and His Resurrection. We dedicate and consecrate all sinners to your Immaculate Heart.

R: *Hail Mary, full of Grace, the Lord is with thee, blessed art thou amongst women and blessed is the fruit of thy womb, Jesus. Holy Mary, Mother of God, pray for us sinners now and at the hour of our death. Amen. Most Sorrowful Mother, Pray for us.*

Final Prayer

Glory to the Father, to the Son, and to the Holy Spirit.

R: *As it was in the beginning, is now, and will be forever. Amen.*

For our Holy Father: Our Father, Who art in heaven,
hallowed be Thy name. Thy kingdom come, Thy will be
done, on earth as it is in heaven. Give us this day our
daily bread, and forgive us our trespasses, as we forgive
those who trespass against us. And lead us not into
temptation but deliver us from evil. Amen.

R: *Hail Mary, full of Grace, the Lord is with thee, blessed art thou
amongst women and blessed is the fruit of thy womb, Jesus.
Holy Mary, Mother of God, pray for us sinners now and at the
hour of our death. Amen. Most Sorrowful Mother, Pray for us.*

Glory to the Father, to the Son, and to the Holy Spirit. As
it was in the beginning, is now, and will be forever.
Amen.

R: *Most Sorrowful Mother, Pray for us.*

THE WAY OF THE CROSS

Opening Prayer

Mary, my Mother, you were the first to live the Way of the
Cross. You felt every pain and every humiliation. You were
unafraid of the ridicule heaped upon you by the crowds. Your
eyes were ever on Jesus and His Pain. Is that the secret of
your miraculous strength? How did your loving heart bear
such a burden and such a weight? As you watched Him stum-
ble and fall, were you tortured by the memory of all the yesterdays—His birth, His hidden life, and His ministry?

You were so desirous of everyone loving Him. What a
heartache it was to see so many hate Him—hate with a dia-

bolical fury. Take my hand as I make this Way of the Cross. Inspire me with those thoughts that will make me realize how much He loves me. Give me light to apply each station to my daily life and to remember my neighbor's needs in this Way of Pain.

Obtain for me the grace to understand the mystery, the wisdom, and the Divine love as I go from scene to scene. Grant that my heart, like yours, may be pierced through by the sight of His sorrow and misery, and that I may determine never to offend Him again. What a price He paid to cover my sins, to open the gates of heaven for me, and to fill my soul with His own Spirit. Sweet Mother, let us travel this way together and grant that the love in my poor heart may give you some slight consolation. Amen.

The First Station: Jesus Is Condemned to Death

My Jesus, the world still has You on trial. It keeps asking who You are and why You make the demands You make. It asks over and over the question, If You are God's Son, why do You permit the world to be in the state it is in? Why are You so silent?

Though the arrogance of the world angers me, I must admit that silently, in the depths of my soul, I too have these questions. Your humility frustrates me and makes me uncomfortable. Your strength before Pilate as You drank deeply from the power of the Father, gives me the answer to my question — the Father's Will. The Father permits many sufferings in my life but it is all for my good. If only I too could be silent in the face of worldly prudence — steadfast in the faith when all seems lost—calm when accused unjustly—free from tyranny of human respect—ready to do the Father's Will no matter how difficult.

Silent Jesus, give us all the graces we need to stand tall in the face of the ridicule of the world. Give the poor the strength not to succumb to their privation but to be ever aware of their dignity as sons of God. Grant that we might not bend to the crippling disease of worldly glory but be willing to be deprived of all things rather than lose Your Friendship. My Jesus, though we are accused daily of being fools, let the vision of Quiet Dignity standing before Monstrous Injustice, give us all the courage to be Your followers. Amen.

The Second Station: Jesus Carries His Cross

How could any human impose such a burden upon Your torn and bleeding Body, Lord Jesus? Each movement of the Cross drove the thorns deeper into Your Head. How did You keep the hatred from welling up in Your Heart? How did the injustice of it all not ruffle Your Peace? The Father's Will was hard on You—why do I complain when it is hard on me?

I see injustice and am frustrated and when my plans to alleviate it seems futile, I despair. When I see those burdened with poverty suffer ever more and cross is added to cross, my heart is far from serene. I utterly fail to see the dignity of the cross as it is carried with love. I would so much rather be without it.

My worldly concept is that suffering, like food, should be shared equally. How ridiculous I am, dear Lord. Just as we do not all need the same amount of material food, neither do we need the same amount of spiritual food and that is what the cross is in my life, isn't it—spiritual food proportional to my needs. Amen.

The Third Station: Jesus Falls the First Time

My Jesus, it seems to me, that as God, You would have carried Your Cross without faltering, but You did not. You fell beneath its weight to show me You understand when I fall. Is it pride that makes me want to shine even in pain? You were not ashamed to fall—to admit the Cross was heavy. There are those in world whom my pride will not tolerate as I want everyone to be strong, yet I am weak. I am ashamed to admit failure in anything.

If the Father permits failure in my life just as He permitted You to fall, then I must know there is good in that failure which my mind will never comprehend. I must not concentrate on the eyes of others as they rest upon me in my falls. Rather, I must reach up to touch that invisible hand and drink in that invisible strength ever at my side.

Weak Jesus, help all men who try so hard to be good but whose nature is constantly opposed to them walking straight and tall down the narrow road of life. Raise their heads to see the glory that is to come rather than the misery of the present moment.

Your Love for me gave You strength to rise from Your fall. Look upon all those whom the world considers unprofitable servants and give them the courage to be more concerned as to how they stand before You, rather than their fellow men. Amen.

The Fourth Station: Jesus Meets His Afflicted Mother

My Jesus, it was a great sorrow to realize Your pain caused Mary so much grief. As Redeemer, You wanted her to share in Your pain for mankind. When You glanced at each other in unutterable suffering, what gave you both the courage to carry on without the least alleviation—without anger at such injustice?

It seems as if You desired to suffer every possible pain to give me an example of how to suffer when my time comes. What a humiliation for You when Your Mother saw You in such a pitiable state—weak, helpless, at the mercy of sinful men—holiness exposed to evil in all hideousness.

Did every moment of that short encounter seem like an eternity? As I see so much suffering in the world, there are times I think it is all hopeless. There is an element of lethargy in my prayers for mankind that says "I'll pray, but what good will it do? The sick grow sicker and the hungry starve." I think of that glance between You and Mary—the glance that said, "Let us give this misery to the Father for the salvation of souls. The Father's power takes our pain and frustration and renews souls, saves them for a new life—a life of eternal joy, eternal happiness. It is worth it all." Give perseverance to the sick so they can carry the cross of frustration and agony with love and resignation for the salvation of others. Amen.

The Fifth Station: Simon Helps Jesus Carry His Cross

My Jesus, Your tormentors enlisted a Simon of Cyrene to help You carry Your Cross. Your Humility is beyond my comprehension. Your Power upheld the whole universe and yet You permit one of Your creatures to help You carry a cross. I imagine Simon was reluctant to take part in Your shame. He had no idea that all who watched and jeered at him would pass into oblivion while his name would go down in history and eternity as the one who helped his God in need. Is it not so with me, dear Jesus? Even when I reluctantly carry my cross as Simon did, it benefits my soul.

If I keep my eyes on You and watch how You suffered, I will be able to bear my cross with greater fortitude. Were you trying to tell all those who suffer from prejudice to have courage? Was Simon a symbol of all those who are hated because of race, color, and creed?

Simon wondered as he took those beams upon his shoulders, why he was chosen for such a heavy burden and now he knows. Help me Jesus, to trust Your loving Providence as You permit suffering to weave itself in and out of my life. Make me understand that You looked at it and held it fondly before You passed it on to me. You watch me and give me strength just as You did Simon. When I enter Your Kingdom, I shall know as he knows, what marvels Your Cross has wrought in my soul. Amen.

The Sixth Station: Veronica Wipes the Face of Jesus

My Jesus, where were all the hundreds of peoples whose bodies and souls were healed by You? Where were they when You needed someone to give You the least sign of comfort? Ingratitude must have borne down upon Your heart and made the cross nearly impossible to carry. There are times I too feel all my efforts for Your Kingdom are futile and end in nothingness. Did Your eyes roam through the crowd for the comfort of just one individual—one sign of pity, one sign of grief?

My heart thrills with a sad joy when I think of one woman, breaking away from fear and human respect and offering You her thin veil to wipe Your bleeding Face. Your Loving Heart, ever watching for the least sign of love, imprinted the Image of Your torn Face upon it! How can You forget Yourself so completely and reward such a small act of kindness?

I must admit, I have been among those who were afraid to know You rather than like Veronica. She did not care if the whole world knew she loved You. Heartbroken Jesus, give me that quality of the soul so necessary to witness to spread Your Word—to tell all people of Your Love for them. Send many into Your Vineyard so the people of all nations may receive the Good News. Imprint Your Divine Image upon my soul and let the thin veil of my human nature bear a perfect resemblance to Your Loving Spirit. Amen.

The Seventh Station: Jesus Falls a Second Time

My Jesus, one of the beautiful qualities the people admired in You was Your Strength in time of ridicule—Your ability to rise above the occasion. But now, You fall a second time— apparently conquered by the pain of the Cross. People who judge You by appearances made a terrible mistake. What looked like weakness was unparalleled strength!

I often judge by the appearance and how wrong I am most of the time. The world judges entirely by this fraudulent method of discerning. It looks down upon those who apparently have given their best and are now in need. It judges the poor as failures, the sick as useless, and the aged as a burden. How wrong that kind of judgment is in the light of Your second fall! Your greatest moment was Your weakest one. Your greatest triumph was in failure. Your greatest act of love was in desolation. Your greatest show of power was in that utter lack of strength that threw You to the ground.

Weak and powerful Jesus, give me the grace to see beyond what is visible and be more aware of Your Wisdom in the midst of weakness. Give the aged, sick, handicapped, retarded, deaf, and blind the fruit of joy so they may ever be aware of the Father's gift and the vast difference between what the world sees and what the Father sees, that they may glory in their weakness so the power of God may be manifest. Amen.

The Eighth Station: Jesus Speaks to the Holy Women

My Jesus, I am amazed at Your Compassion for others in Your time of need. When I suffer, I have a tendency to think only of myself but You forgot Yourself completely. When You saw the holy women weeping over Your torments, You consoled them and taught them to look deeper into Your Passion. You wanted them to understand that the real evil to cry over was the rejection You suffered from the Chosen people—a people set apart from every other nation, who refused to accept God's Son.

The Act of Redemption would go on and no one would ever be able to take away Your Dignity as Son of God, but the evil, greed, jealousy, and ambition in the hearts of those who should have recognized You was the issue to grieve over. To be so close to God made man and miss Him completely was the real crime.

My Jesus, I fear I do the same when I strain gnats and then swallow camels—when I take out the splinter in my brother's eye and forget the beam in my own. It is such a gift— this gift of faith. It is such a sublime grace to possess Your own Spirit. Why haven't I advanced in holiness of life? I miss the many disguises you take upon Yourself and see only people, circumstances, and human events, not the loving hand of the Father guiding all things. Help all those who are discouraged, sick, lonely, and old to recognize Your Presence in their midst. Amen.

The Ninth Station: Jesus Falls the Third Time

My Jesus, even with the help of Simon You fell a third time. Were You telling me that there may be times in my life that I will fall again and again despite the help of friends and loved ones? There are times when the crosses You permit in my life are more than I can bear. It is as if all the sufferings of a lifetime are suddenly compressed into the present moment and it is more than I can stand.

Though it grieves my heart to see You so weak and helpless, it is a comfort to my soul to know that you understand my sufferings from Your own experience. Your Love for me made You want to experience every kind of pain just so I could have someone to look to for example and courage.

When I cry out from the depths of my soul, "This suffering is more than I can bear," do You whisper, "Yes, I understand"? When I am discouraged after many falls, do You say in my innermost being, "Keep going, I know how hard it is to rise"?

There are many people who are sorely tried in body and soul with alcohol and drug weaknesses who try and try and fall again and again. Through the humiliation of this third fall, give them the courage and perseverance to take up their cross and follow You. Amen.

The Tenth Station: Jesus Is Stripped of His Garments

It seems that every step to Calvary brought You fresh humiliation, my Jesus. How Your sensitive nature recoiled at being stripped before a crowd of people. You desired to leave this life as You entered it—completely detached from all the comforts of this world. You want me to know without a doubt that You loved me with an unselfish love. Your love for me caused You nothing but pain and sorrow. You gave everything and received nothing in return. Why do I find it so hard to be detached?

In your loving mind, dear Jesus, did You look up to the Father as You stood there on that windy hill, shivering from cold and shame and trembling from fear, and ask Him to have mercy on those who would violate their purity and make love a mockery? Did You ask forgiveness for those whose greed would make them lie, cheat, and steal for a few pieces of cold silver?

Forgive us all, dear Jesus. Look upon the world with pity, for mankind has lost its way and the principles of this world make lust a fun game and luxury a necessity. Detachment has become merely another hardship of the poor and obedience the fault of the weak. Have mercy on us and grant the people of this day the courage to see and know themselves and the light to change. Amen.

The Eleventh Station: Jesus Is Nailed to the Cross

It is hard to imagine a God being nailed to a cross by His Own creatures. It is even more difficult for my mind to understand a love that permitted such a thing to happen! As those men drove heavy nails into Your hands and feet, dear Jesus, did You offer the pain as reparation for some particular human weakness and sin? Was the nail in Your right hand for those who spend their lives in dissipation and boredom?

Was the nail in Your left hand in reparation for all consecrated souls who live lukewarm lives? Were You stretching out Your arms to show us how much You love us? As the feet that walked the hot, dusty roads were nailed fast, did they cramp up in a deadly grip of pain to make reparation for all those who so nimbly run the broad road of sin and self-indulgence?

It seems, dear Jesus, Your love has held You bound hand and foot as Your heart pleads for a return of love. You seem to shout from the top of the hill "I love you — come to me — see, I am held fast — I cannot hurt you — only you can hurt Me." How very hard is the heart that can see such love and turn away. Is it not true I too have turned away when I did not accept the Father's Will with love? Teach me to keep my arms ever open to love, to forgive and to render service — willing to be hurt rather than hurt, satisfied to love and not be loved in return. Amen.

The Twelfth Station: Jesus Dies on the Cross

God is dead! No wonder the earth quaked, the sun hid itself, the dead rose, and Mary stood by in horror. Your human body gave up its soul in death but Your Divinity, dear Jesus, continued to manifest its power. All creation rebelled as the Word made Flesh departed from this world. Man alone was too proud to see and too stubborn to acknowledge truth.

Redemption was accomplished! Man would never have

an excuse to forget how much You loved him. The thief on Your right saw something he could not explain—he saw a man on a tree and knew He was God. His need made him see his own guilt and Your innocence. The Promise of eternal life made the remaining hours of his torture endurable.

A common thief responded to Your love with deep Faith, Hope, and Love. He saw more than his eyes envisioned—he felt a Presence he could not explain and would not argue with. He was in need and accepted the way God designed to help him.

Forgive our pride, dear Jesus, as we spend hours speculating, days arguing, and often a lifetime in rejecting Your death, which is a sublime mystery. Have pity on those whose intelligence leads them to pride because they never feel the need to reach out to the Man of Sorrows for consolation. Amen.

The Thirteenth Station:
Jesus Is Taken Down from the Cross

My Jesus, it was with deep grief that Mary finally took You into her arms and saw all the wounds sin had inflicted upon You. Mary Magdalene looked upon Your dead Body with horror. Nicodemus, the man so full of human respect, who came to You by night, suddenly received the courage to help Joseph take you down from the Cross. You are once more surrounded by only a few followers. When loneliness and failure cross my path, let me think of this lonely moment and this total failure—failure in the eyes of men. How wrong they were—how mistaken their concept of success! The greatest act of love was given in desolation and the most successful mission accomplished and finished when all seemed lost. Is this not true in my life, dear Jesus? I judge my failures harshly. I demand perfection instead of holiness. My idea of success is for all to end well—according to my liking.

Give to all men the grace to see that doing Your Will is more important than success. If failure is permitted for my greater good then teach me how to use it to my advantage. Let me say as You once said, that to do the Will of the Father is my food. Let not the standards of this world take possession of me or destroy the good You have set for me—to be Holy and to accomplish the Father's Will with great love. Let me accept praise or blame, success or failure with equal serenity. Amen.

The Fourteenth Station: Jesus Is Laid in the Sepulcher

My Jesus, You were laid to rest in a stranger's tomb. You were born with nothing of this world's goods and You died detached from everything. When You came into the world, men slept and Angels sang and now as You leave it, Creation is silent and only a few weep. Both events were clothed in obscurity. The majority of men live in such a way. Most of us live and die knowing and known by only a few. Were You trying to tell us, dear Jesus, how very important our lives are just because we are accomplishing the Father's Will? Will we ever learn the lesson of humility that makes us content with who we are, where we are, and what we are?

Will our Faith ever be strong enough to see power in

weakness and good in the sufferings of our lives? Will our Hope be trusting enough to rely on Your Providence even when we have nowhere to lay our head? Will our Love ever be strong enough not to take scandal in the cross?

My Jesus, hide my soul in Your Heart as You lie in the sepulcher alone. Let my heart be as a fire to keep you warm. Let my desire to know and love You be like a torch to light up the darkness. Let my soul sing softly a hymn of repentant love as the hours pass and Your Resurrection is at hand. Let me rejoice, dear Jesus, with all the Angels in a hymn of praise and thanksgiving for so great a love—so great a God—so great a day! Amen.

Closing Prayer

My Jesus, I have traveled Your Way of the cross. It seems so real and I feel so ashamed. I complain of my sufferings and find obedience to the Father's Will difficult. My mind bogged down by the poverty, sickness, starvation, greed, and hatred in the world. There are many innocent people who suffer so unjustly. There are those born with physical and mental defects. Do we understand that You continue to carry Your Cross in the minds and bodies of each human being? Help me to see the Father's Will in every incident of my daily life. This is what You did—You saw the Father's Will in Your persecutors, Your enemies, and Your pain. You saw a beauty in the Cross and embraced it as a desired treasure. My worldly mind is dulled by injustice and suffering and I lose sight of the glory that is to come. Help me to trust the Father and to realize that there is something great behind the most insignificant suffering.

There is Someone lifting my cross to fit my shoulders—there is Divine Wisdom in all the petty annoyances that irk my soul every day. Teach me the lessons contained in my cross, the wisdom of its necessity, the beauty of its variety, and the fortitude that accompanies even the smallest cross. Mary, my Mother, obtain for me the grace to be Jesus to my neighbor and to see my neighbor in Jesus. Amen.

> If any soul would develop a habit of being aware of the Father within it, loving Jesus in every human being the soul meets—would not that soul make giant strides in holiness? Would it not look upon everyone with new eyes and new love? Would it not treat everyone as Jesus?
>
> —*Mother Angelica*

A Prayer to Jesus Crucified

O Jesus, Who, through Thy Burning Love for us didst will to be nailed to the Cross and to shed Thy Precious Blood for the redemption and salvation of our souls, look upon us who, fully trusting in Thy Mercy, are here gathered together in the remembrance of Thy Most Sorrowful Passion and Death: purify us, by Thy Grace, from sin; hallow our labor; give unto us and all our dear ones our daily bread; sweeten our sorrows; bless our families; and grant unto the nations that are so sorely afflicted Thy Peace, which is the only true peace, in order that we, being obedient to Thy Commandments, may attain unto heavenly glory. Amen.

The faithful who, being at least contrite, devoutly recite this prayer on Good Friday at three o'clock, the hour at which our LORD Jesus Christ expired on the Cross, may gain an indulgence of five hundred days.

Into Thy hands, O Lord, I commend my spirit. (PCPA Prayer Book)

Prayer to the Shoulder Wound of Our Lord Jesus

This prayer was among Rita Rizzo's earliest devotions. Mother Angelica said: "Before I entered the cloister, I had great devotion to the wound on the Lord's left shoulder. I passed out copies of this devotion and on the back of the prayer cards I would write: 'If you want more of this, write to Rita [Rizzo].' That devotion had tremendous promises attached to it . . . oh the indulgences attached to devotion of the left shoulder of Jesus!" According to tradition, St. Bernard of Clairvaux was told by Jesus that the wound on His left shoulder was more painful than any other. The Lord promised to remit the venial sins and forget the mortal sins of all those who venerated His wound. Pope Eugenius III, at St. Bernard's urging, granted a three-thousand-year indulgence to anyone who recited the Lord's Prayer and three Hail Mary's in honor of the wound where Christ shouldered the cross.

O Loving Jesus, meek Lamb of God, I, a miserable sinner, salute and worship the most Sacred Wound of Thy Shoulder on which Thou didst bear Thy heavy Cross, which so tore Thy Flesh and laid bare Thy Bones as to inflict on Thee an anguish greater than any other wound of Thy Most Blessed Body. I adore Thee, O Jesus, most sorrowful; I praise and glorify Thee, and give Thee thanks for this most sacred and painful Wound, beseeching Thee by that exceeding pain, and by the crushing burden of Thy heavy Cross, to be merciful to me, a sinner, to forgive me all my mortal and venial sins, and to lead me on toward Heaven along the Way of Thy Cross. Amen.

Say one Our Father and three Hail Marys.

The Divine Mercy Chaplet

In the year 2000 Pope John Paul II made Sr. Faustina Kowalska a saint. In the doing, he established the Sunday after Easter as Divine Mercy Sunday, elevating the Divine Mercy Chaplet given to Faustina and her message to universal status. Mother Angelica had been promoting the chaplet via daily television broadcasts since 1996. It is prayed on the rosary. According to Sr. Faustina's diary, the Lord told her:

> *Say unceasingly this chaplet that I have taught you. Anyone who says it will receive great Mercy at the hour of death. Priests will recommend it to sinners as the last hope. Even the most hardened sinner, if he recites this Chaplet even once, will receive grace from My Infinite Mercy. I*

want the whole world to know My Infinite Mercy. I want to give unimaginable graces to those who trust in My Mercy.

1. Begin with the Sign of the Cross, an Our Father, a Hail Mary, and the Apostles Creed.
2. Then on the Our Father beads say the following:

Eternal Father, I offer You the Body and Blood, Soul and Divinity of Your dearly beloved Son, Our Lord Jesus Christ, in atonement for our sins and those of the whole world.

3. On the ten Hail Mary beads say the following:

For the sake of His sorrowful Passion, have mercy on us and on the whole world.

(Repeat steps 2 and 3 for all five decades.)

4. Conclude by reciting three times:

Holy God, Holy Mighty One, Holy Immortal One, have mercy on us and on the whole world.

CONSECRATION TO THE IMMACULATE HEART OF MARY

Mother Angelica always had a strong devotion to Mary, the Mother of God. She instructed her sisters: "Keep your heart with Our Lady. It's full of love for you. We're all going to suffer something, and this may be the time for you. But don't let anything that happens dishearten you or cause you to lose faith in Jesus, or the Father, or the Spirit. Run to your Mother, run to Our Lady, enter this garden of love.

"Look at what Our Lady told a mystic: 'Enter into My Immaculate Heart so you may feel the force and the tenderness of My Motherly love for you. Through your consecration to My Immaculate Heart you enter into a safe refuge.' A safe refuge. Aren't we all looking for that in these days of uncertainty? Oh, it's such a wonderful time to be alive. In these times I think it's important that you live this consecration. And it doesn't matter whether you're Catholic or not. We're asking the Mother of God to intercede with Jesus for us. We're putting ourselves in Her heart, under Her protection against the enemy who has been let loose and is showing his face. Our Lady will keep Her promise. Her Immaculate Heart will triumph."

O Mary, Virgin Most Powerful, and Mother of Mercy, Queen of Heaven, and Refuge of sinners, I consecrate myself to Your Immaculate Heart. I consecrate my being and my life, all that I have, all that I am, and all that I love. To You I give my body, my heart, and my soul. To You I give my home, my family, and my country. I desire that everything in me, everything around me, belong to You. To make this act of consecration purposeful and lasting I renew this day, at this time my promises of baptism. Finally, O Glorious Mother of God and Loving Mother, I promise I shall try to inspire in others the devotion to You so as to hasten, through the Queenship of Your Immaculate Heart, the coming kingdom of the Sacred Heart. Amen.

The Rosary from the Heart

PRAYING THE ROSARY FROM THE HEART

Mother Angelica deeply loved the Rosary. She once taught her nuns to pray it, not by rote, but "from the heart." Here is a lesson on the topic from 1999, followed by her personal meditations on the mysteries of the Rosary.

The Rosary is so powerful. Designed by Our Lady, and commanded by God Himself it is the most powerful prayer after the liturgy and the Divine Office. Every mystery is the cause of a giant step forward in holiness. We should make an effort to say three Rosaries a day. Because it's really necessary for me to go through the life of Jesus, be it ever so fast, because in doing so I am being filled with the Eternal Word. A combination of mental prayer and vocal prayer, the Rosary is for everybody. The problem we often have is: We either meditate on it or pray it aloud, but we're seemingly not able to combine the two. Now, you could just pronounce the prayers, but if you are not meditating upon the mysteries, you are missing half of the grace.

Don't tell me you can't meditate because you do it every day. I'm here knocking myself out talking and some of you have that starry-eyed look. You hear what I'm saying—some of you can even respond—but your mind is meditating on something entirely different. Have you any idea how much time we waste just wondering about things? You're in some other place.

That's one of our major problems: Our mind is like a runaway horse. We have no mental discipline. If you're going to use the graces of the present moment, you have to have mental discipline, which means as soon as you are aware that your mind has wandered into useless, barren territory (and anything that is not of God, or for God, is barren territory) return to Our Lady and Our Lord. We never reach serenity of soul, because our minds are busy with everything but God. We need to turn that imagination over to the Lord and focus on Him. And don't tell me you can't meditate on the Rosary and say the Hail Mary at the same time. You do two things at once all the time. The Rosary should be prayed from the heart.

When I say the Rosary I allow my soul to gaze at God with great love and admiration; to gaze at the particular mystery. You can take any mystery from the Joyful to the Glorious and admire the perfection of Our Lady or an attribute of God. For instance, look at the Visitation: It's admirable that Our Lady would go to see Elizabeth immediately. Her union with God's Will was awesome. She told St. Joseph that they should go to Elizabeth, and off they went. You could consider that for at least twenty Hail Mary's. And even after you pass the mystery, you can still admire that perfection in Our Lady or that attribute in God. That's prayer of the heart because you're not reasoning, you're simply gazing upon some admirable attribute or perfection in Our Lady. It's awesome to say the Rosary that way because *you* are not in it at all. This prayer of the heart goes beyond ourselves and we are free to admire the Lord, or Our Lady, or God the Father.

If you're not making progress in one virtue, say your Rosary and meditate on that virtue as Our Lord practiced it. I cannot get over my faults and weaknesses if I don't substitute those faults and weaknesses for something of God. This is precisely why the life of Jesus and the reading of Scripture and the Rosary never seem to change us—why we remain the same: Because to change you need to admire someone other than yourself.

It's all right to get fixed on one mystery. Consider the mystery deeply and pick one aspect of it to meditate upon.

For instance if the mystery is the Annunciation: Our Lady says, "Be it done to me according to Thy Word." Well, do I do that? If you want to use your reason, see Our Lady there, see the angel, look at Our Lady's face with great admiration. That's a meditation.

Personally, when I meditate on the first mystery, I've always felt that not a leaf on a tree moved. The wind stopped, the birds didn't sing, the waves were very soft. Even in nature, there was a kind of awesome expectation. Then, she said, "Be it done unto me according to Thy Word." At that moment I think all the waves crashed, the birds twittered in a whole different way, and the Angels sang, "Alleluia! He's coming." Suddenly, the Eternal Word came down. All of that came from one mystery, the Annunciation. The Lord Himself said, "Behold your Mother"—well this is your chance.

Forget your mind. Forget your reason. Just admire Our Lady during the Rosary. Admire God for doing the miraculous—the impossible.

The Apostles Creed
(Recited once at the beginning of the Rosary)

I believe in God, the Father Almighty, Creator of Heaven and earth; and in Jesus Christ, His only Son, our Lord; who was conceived by the Holy Spirit, born of the Virgin Mary, suffered under Pontius Pilate, was crucified, died, and was buried. He descended into hell; the third day He arose again from the dead; He ascended into heaven, sitteth at the right hand of God, the Father Almighty from thence He shall come to judge the living and the dead. I believe in the Holy Spirit, the Holy Catholic Church, the communion of saints, the forgiveness of sins, the resurrection of the body, and life everlasting. Amen.

The Our Father (Recited before each mystery)

Our Father, who art in heaven, hallowed by Thy Name; Thy kingdom come; Thy will be done on earth as it is in heaven. Give us this day our daily bread, and forgive us our trespasses as we forgive those who trespass against us; and lead us not into temptation, but deliver us from evil. Amen.

The Hail Mary (Recited ten times following each mystery)

Hail Mary, full of grace! The Lord is with thee; blessed art thou among women, and blessed is the fruit of thy womb, Jesus. Holy Mary, Mother of God, pray for us sinners now and at the hour of our death. Amen.

Glory be to the Father
(Recited once after the ten Hail Marys)

Glory be to the Father, and to the Son, and to the Holy Spirit. As it was in the beginning, is now, and ever shall be, world without end. Amen.

The Hail Holy Queen
(Recited once at the conclusion of the Rosary)

Hail! Holy Queen, Mother of Mercy, our life, our sweetness, and our hope. To thee do we cry, poor banished children of Eve. To thee do we send up our sighs, mourning and weeping in this valley of tears. Turn then, O most gracious advocate, thine eyes of mercy toward us; and after this our exile, show unto us the blessed fruit of thy womb, Jesus. O clement! O Loving! O sweet Virgin Mary! Pray for us, O Holy Mother of God. That we may be made worthy of the promises of Christ. Amen.

THE JOYFUL MYSTERIES

The Annunciation

Hail, full of grace, the Lord is with thee. Blessed art thou among women.

—Luke 1:28

This is the first time we meet Our Lady. In the Annunciation, we see her two great virtues: faith and obedience. Put yourself in Our Lady's place for a minute. You had decided to live a virginal life—and you can imagine the intensity with which Our Lady would have wished to live in this manner. Then suddenly, even though it's an angel who says, "This is the will of God," there has to be in Our Lady a total change of mind and heart. In this most difficult request she faces a radical change of life.

You've got to keep in mind her absolute holiness, her absolute dedication to God. Some say that would have made it easy. Not so, because she had to give up her plans—become something she could not even fathom. Once she knew how she would conceive and bear a Son, which was her right as a woman, she said, "Let it be done unto me according to Thy Word." What an absolutely phenomenal passage of Scripture. It gives us an idea of what it means to be full of grace. We can well measure the grace in our hearts and souls by our obedience to God's will in the present moment. It's that immediate response of "Yes" to whatever the Lord asks. So we find in Our Lady a very unusual woman from the beginning. She was least twelve years old, maybe fourteen—and what obedience she showed. What a tremendous amount of holiness she had. Why can't we trust God's plan in our lives as she trusted Him?

Give us a share of your faith and hope, dear Mother, that we may bow before the Infinite Wisdom of God and accept the treasures He deigns to bestow upon us. Let us leave creation to His Omnipotence; the future to His Providence; and mankind to His Wisdom.

Pray ten Hail Marys and one Glory Be.

The Visitation

When Elizabeth heard the greeting of Mary the babe in her womb leapt, and she was filled with the Holy Spirit.
—*Luke 1:41*

We look at Mary now at the Visitation, and we find the most unusual thing happened. When we have some kind of consolation from God—when you experience His presence in the chapel, say—your whole desire is to just sit there for as long as possible. You just want to enjoy and savor the Lord's Presence. What is most unusual about Our Lady is she doesn't act that way. After this amazing infusion of the Eternal Word she gets up "in haste," it says, and goes to visit her cousin Elizabeth. It wasn't very far in distance, about five miles or so, but it was very mountainous and uphill. St. Joseph must have brought her there. For Our Lady this had to be a tremendous sacrifice. She very likely spent a night in prayer or a day savoring this tremendous gift: that she was to be the mother of the Messiah. Then she took off. We see that the reality of charity was uppermost in Our Lady's mind. Not even her own great gift could stand in the way of charity—that love she had for her cousin. I'm sure Our Lady knew also, because it was revealed to her, that she had a mission. Evangelization began at the Visitation. She must have known that her Son would sanctify John in Elizabeth's womb. It was necessary that John be sanctified as soon as possible. I'm sure that's why she made haste.

Dear Mother, your zeal to carry Jesus to others, no matter the cost, embarrasses us and causes us to blush with shame. Holy Mary, bring Jesus to us through the merits of your visit to Elizabeth. Obtain for us the graces we need to magnify the Lord by our humility in dealing with our neighbor, our concern for the aged, our zeal for social justice, and our courage when duty calls for sacrifice.

Pray ten Hail Marys and one Glory Be.

The Nativity

And she brought forth her first-born Son and wrapped Him in swaddling clothes.

—Luke 2:7

We see Our Lady at the Nativity and St. Joseph, who is rightfully depressed. He couldn't provide something for his wife. She was with child, obviously close to the time of delivery, and he could find no room for them. Our Lord allowed Mary to suffer on a human level so that she could bring forth that heroic virtue. Our Lady had to practice heroic virtue far beyond anything asked of us. She was so absolutely, totally united to God's will that she saw God in what was happening.

They couldn't find anything but a cave. It was cold and windy outside, so they made use of what they had in serenity.

There's no woman born in sin who would understand and be happy with this situation. But there she was, with the Son of God, the Redeemer of the world, the Eternal Word in a stable. You can imagine the adoration and praise Our Lady gave the Eternal Word made man. The Angels must have been absolutely floored because they knew that God had a right to determine the circumstances of his coming—but the details were unknown to them. Never in a million years would they have imagined not only that He would become man, but that God would be so lowly a man—born in a stable. The Angels knew His Grandeur, His Majesty, His Awesomeness, His Power. His Humility and Simplicity is something they and the entire world did not expect.

Sweet Mother, obtain for us the grace to see Jesus in the lowly and offer Jesus to the forgotten. Teach us how to be holy, so we may give the Father the glory and Jesus the pleasure of making sinners into saints.

Pray ten Hail Marys and one Glory Be.

The Presentation

According to the law of Moses, they took Jesus up to Jerusalem to present Him to the Lord.

—Luke 2:32

We see Our Lady at the Presentation. Imagine the humiliation of this. She had to be purified and our Blessed Lord presented in the temple. She had to wait forty days because she was considered to be like every other woman going up the temple steps. No one would even think that a woman in their midst had conceived a child and remained a virgin. She proceeded up the steps like all the other women. Now we see her absolute humility and we also see the sword of sorrow. What new mother wants to hear that their baby has been born for a specific reason, and the reason is for "the fall and the rising of many in Israel." The fall! From the time Jesus arrived, people either received Him or they didn't. If you didn't, it was a fall; if you did, you were raised up. Simeon tells Mary, "A sword shall pierce your own soul." Oh God, you can't even imagine that. Our Lord allowed Our Lady to grow into the Cross. It didn't just come upon her all at once. First, He's born in a stable and then He goes up into the temple. Two prophets acknowledge His dignity, but they give His Mother this bittersweet message.

Holy Mother, the Child of your womb was destined to be great but how few recognized that greatness. Give the parents of special children a deep realization of the power of their suffering. Let their suffering rise to heaven as a sweet-smelling incense for the salvation of souls. Let the beauty of their souls, hidden from the eyes of men in this life, shine like bright stars in the glory of the Father's Kingdom.

Pray ten Hail Marys and one Glory Be.

Finding the Child Jesus in the Temple

After three days they found Him in the Temple. He was sitting in the midst of the teachers.

—Luke 2:45, 46

You can imagine our Lord arriving at the temple at twelve years of age. It's a long time between incidents in the Scriptures. At this moment Our Lady experiences what everyone in the spiritual life must endure. There has to be a cross in our life. There has to be that feeling of absolute desolation and a sense of loss—otherwise our hearts and souls cannot raise themselves up to God in complete abandonment and purity. Our Lady and St. Joseph become separated from Jesus. They journey back to Jerusalem without the slightest idea of where to look for Him. Mary of Agreda tells us that Mary and Joseph wandered through the streets, day and night, blaming themselves. Our Lady's great fear was that someone recognized the Lord and harmed Him before His time—and it would be her fault. What a terrible dark night of the soul: that feeling that you were given a mission and you failed to fulfill it. That's why when she finds our Lord you can almost hear the frustration in Our Lady's voice: "My child, why have you done this to us? See how worried your father and I have been, looking for you." Our Lord looks at her in wonderment and says, "Did you not know that I must be busy with My Father's affairs?" He was beginning to teach the doctors of the church. He was giving them the opportunity to think about the coming of the Messiah. And they were "astounded at his knowledge."

But for Our Lady the separation from Jesus was a profound trial. At that point, the Scripture says He was obedient to Mary and Joseph. Our Lady pondered all these things in her heart.

Dear Lady, obtain for our families a deeper union with

the Trinity. Make the father head, the mother heart, and the children members of one another. When the sword of separation in mind, heart, or ideals tears the family apart, grant that the healing balm of love may find them in the Temple of God's Will, listening to His voice speaking of harmony in the depths of their souls.

Pray ten Hail Marys and one Glory Be.

THE SORROWFUL MYSTERIES

The Agony in the Garden

Jesus came with them to Gethsemane and He began to be saddened and exceedingly troubled.

—Matthew 26:36, 37

During Our Lord's Agony in the Garden, His Mother surely knew what was happening. In this moment we see her heroic virtue again. Our Lady's self-control is phenomenal. She did not run into the garden and comfort her Son. She knew her place of suffering, and if He was going to feel abandoned, so would she feel abandoned. The Will of God was so preeminent in her mind, just as it was in the mind of Jesus. It was not the Father's Will that she go into the garden and kneel next to Jesus and console Him. Her suffering was doubled by the fact that she couldn't be there with Him. For in that garden the Lord saw the sufferings to come and shuddered with fear, utterly alone. He begged the Father to let the chalice pass from Him.

Dear Lord, Your example of resignation, acceptance, and love makes me realize that the Father has my life in His hands and nothing happens to me that is not for my good. Give me the confidence to ask for what I think I need, the humility to wait for His Will, and the faith to accept a refusal. Let my suffering be Redemptive, let my will be one with God's, and my life a sacrifice of love.

Pray ten Hail Marys and one Glory Be.

The Scourging of Our Lord

Pilate then took Jesus and had Him scourged.

—John 19:1

We can't imagine Our Lady at the scourging of Jesus. Mary of Agreda says that she felt each lash in her body. This makes sense because how many mystics throughout the centuries have felt those wounds, that scourging, and bled? We know of St. Francis, Padre Pio, Mrs. Wise [a mystic Mother knew as a young woman]. So it stands to reason that if these holy people suffered with Our Lord, how much more would His Mother suffer? There's no mystical grace, no virtue, no pain, no suffering that she was denied. Otherwise, she couldn't understand what we endure and truly be our mother.

With Mary nearby, Our Lord was mercilessly beaten, stripped of all dignity, and whipped like an animal. Innocence was torn apart by wicked men.

Surely, my Jesus, this scourging made reparation for

more than the sins of the flesh. Were the welts suffered for those who tear off the garments of love and clothe themselves in the rags of dissension and disobedience? Was one lash marked "Rudeness" and another "Hate"? And when the scourging finally ended, did Your eyes see some blood trickling down and stepped upon as if in derision? We are sorry, dear Jesus. Cover us all with this Precious Blood and heal our many wounds. Let modesty and purity be our goal and harmony our motto.

Pray ten Hail Marys and one Glory Be.

Crowning with Thorns

And plaiting a crown of thorns they put it upon His head and a reed in His right hand.

—Matthew 27:29

In the Crowning of Thorns, our Lord made reparation for pride, for all of the evil perpetrated in the human mind. Remember, He said if you look at a woman with lust, you've already committed adultery. He called the memory a storehouse from whence comes evil. He made reparation for those who fill their memory with hate, anger, guilt; the things that prevent us from growth. He made reparation for all the resentments we carry for events or people, for our lack of charity: the criticism, selfishness, cynicism, pettiness—all of the things in the will. In the Crowning of Thorns He repaired and suffered for all these sins. Not only did Our Lady suffer the pains herself, but she would have been praying for all of those people who somehow or other are oblivious of wrongdoing or oblivious of sin, for those who are obstinate in their will. People like the Pharisees and us.

When I consider the Crowning of Thorns I need to understand how serious it is when I sin with my mind. Sometimes you don't sin outwardly, but you do sin with your mind.

The real crown of thorns were not little bitty things. They were long, like nails. Looking on, Our Lady would have had a tremendous amount of empathy for the Lord, but also for those who glibly sin without considering the consequences or what it cost the Lord.

Dear Jesus, were the thorns that pricked Your Head the worries I permit to choke Your Word from my mind? Were the resentments I cherish in my memory the reed that struck Your Head? And when the spittle ran down Your Face, did my arrogance make You cry? Oh, Jesus, let me never forget Your Love for me and the reparation You offered the Father for my sake. Let my soul magnify the Lord by humility of heart, purity of mind, and a gentle spirit.

Pray ten Hail Marys and one Glory Be.

Carrying of the Cross

And bearing the Cross for Himself, He went forth to the place called The Skull.

—John 19:17

The Romans had various ways they made people carry crosses. Most of the time it was a horizontal beam. They used to have so many crucifixions that they kept the vertical beam at the crucifixion site. The prisoner would have to carry the horizontal beam on his shoulders, around his waist would be a rope which the soldiers would pull to deliberately make the condemned fall. Some mystic I read not too long ago said that Our Lord's left knee was completely torn up because of constant falling on it. His shoulders and the Body that carried this tremendous beam was already scourged and crowned with thorns. So, this wasn't a healthy body—which was the norm for prisoners. There was that deep hatred for Jesus as God-man. So He had to go through all of these tortures to make specific reparation to the Father for our sins.

Imagine Our Lady, when she saw that beam literally being thrown on Jesus' devastated shoulders. We need to think of the Passion of Jesus and Mary, who knew of the sins borne on that horizontal log. It wasn't just the weight of the plank; it was the weight of sin. Our Lady would have grieved for all the sins of today and all the sins and atrocities throughout the centuries that were on that plank. So she would be carrying not only the burden of the Cross as Jesus did, she would be carrying the terror of sin—the horror of sin.

Help me, my Jesus, to carry my cross with joy, ever keeping my eyes on the Father's Will. Grant that I may not waste time deciding which cross comes from You and which comes from my neighbor. Let me accept all from You, realizing that some crosses correct me, some release me, some prevent me from a life of sin, others are redemptive, and still others lead to repentance. May our cross be one cross, dear Jesus, that together we may glorify the Father and save souls.

Pray ten Hail Marys and one Glory Be.

The Crucifixion of Jesus

And when they came to the place called the Skull they crucified Him.

—Luke 23:33

When Our Lord finally got up the hill, the terror really began. If you read accounts of various mystics, it sends shivers up your spine. Most criminals were tied up there with ropes. It was very seldom that someone was nailed to a cross, unless he was a terrible, terrible criminal. Our Lord was a terrible criminal, because He took upon Himself our sins. And all the while His Mother is there. Even if she wasn't looking, imagine hearing a hammer nail someone you love to a cross. The sound alone would drive you mad. But Our Lady was very strong. She knew why Our Dear Lord was suffering like that. She must have followed Him everywhere, and again, she felt what He felt on that awful day: when people denied Him, when they jeered and booed at His words, when the nails pierced His flesh. Now she has to see the end. He lost so much blood from the scourging and the falls, it has to be a miracle that He was able to endure six solid hours on the cross. According to the Scripture, He was nailed to the cross at nine in the morning and He didn't die until three in the afternoon. What a terrible agony. Our Lady had to watch Him gasp for breath, pulling Himself up on His nailed feet to speak. I imagine that she encouraged Him. She knew what was at stake: the redemption of the world, of you.

The seven last words of Jesus must have been like seven swords for Our Lady because when someone you love is agonizing, struggling to speak, it is painful. It must have been terrible for Our Lady to hear Him say, "I thirst" when she loved Him with her whole Immaculate Heart. I think if there were any consoling words among the last ones, it would be "Father forgive them, they know not what they do." What a heroic kind of forgiveness. Our Lady would have repeated that as she watched Jesus breathe his last.

Help me, Jesus, to see Your loving gaze as it looked up to the Father with abandonment, at the thief with mercy, and at Your Mother with love. Grant that I may forgive my enemies and abandon myself to the Father's Will. Let me commend my life and my eternity to His care. Let zeal for the salvation of souls make my soul thirst for sacrifice and let the thought of paradise enlighten my path.

Give me the grace to persevere to the end, and when the journey is over and I have fought the good fight, let the Angels sing the last verse of my earthly song: "It is finished."

Pray ten Hail Marys and one Glory Be.

THE GLORIOUS MYSTERIES

The Resurrection of Jesus

He is not here, but has risen. Behold the place where they laid Him.

—Luke 24:6; Mark 16:6

The tomb was empty on that Resurrection morning. Mary the mother of James and Mary Magdalene went to visit the sepulcher, and the Angels said to them "Why look among the dead for Someone who is alive?" Don't we do the same today? Don't we seek hope and answers among the dead—among those who have forsaken God and his ways? What does the Angel say? "He is not here. He has risen."

Lord, the joy of Your Resurrection fills my soul with exultation and the realization that my body, too, will rise someday. Like Your Five Wounds, my suffering will also shine for all to see. The Wisdom of the Father will be glorified forever as all men see how His Plan and Will in my life marked out the glory that would be mine for all eternity.

All the trials, sufferings, heartaches, and disappointments will seem as nothing compared to the glory Your sufferings merited for me. They shall all seem like a dream, and the vision of Your face will fill my soul with exquisite joy. My soul, reunited to my body, will be perfect as Yours is perfect. No evil tendencies will ever again disturb it, no weakness mar its beauty, no separations grieve my soul, no sickness or tears shatter my peace, no regrets cloud my mind.

I will love and be loved by everyone and nothing will be impossible for me. The Father will be ever at my side and together with You, dear Jesus, I will roam freely in love of the Spirit forever and ever.

Pray ten Hail Marys and one Glory Be.

The Ascension of Jesus

And He was taken up into Heaven and sits at the Right Hand of God.

—Mark 16:19

St. Matthew tells us: "The eleven disciples set out for Galilee to the mountain where Jesus had arranged to meet them. And when they saw Him they fell down before Him, though some hesitated." Like the Apostles, I think there's something wrong with all of us. We hesitate as well! The Apostles saw Him die, they saw Him crucified, they saw Him rise from the dead. After he rose they walked with Him, ate with Him — He made them breakfast at the Sea of Tiberius. He stayed with them for forty days. Now, wouldn't you think that'd be enough? Still some "knelt" and some "hesitated." The Lord told them, "All authority in Heaven and earth has been given to Me. Go, therefore, and make disciples of all nations and baptize them in the Name of the Father and the Son and the Holy Spirit and know that I AM with you always, even to the end of time."

Even though we see Jesus seemingly leave us, He is with us "to the end of time."

Dear Jesus, I find the day You ascended to the Father a sad day. It resembles my soul when, after experiencing Your Presence, it is plunged into a state of dryness. Like the Apostles I tend to stand still and look up in the hope that I will once again experience the joy of Your Presence. When this happens, my Lord, remind me of the Angels' admonition, "Why do you stand here idle looking up to Heaven?"

This dryness of soul is something I must work with and not against. Help me to realize that when I feel Your Presence You are consoling me, but when I do not feel that Presence and I continue a life of love and virtue, I am consoling You. Teach me to prefer consoling You to being consoled, and give me the light to exercise my Faith when all seems dark.

I want to rise above the demands of my emotions and have the courage to live in spirit and truth—and never hesitate. Grant me the Faith that is always aware of the invisible reality, the Hope that trusts in Your promises, and the Love that seeks not itself.

Pray ten Hail Marys and one Glory Be.

The Descent of the Holy Spirit

And suddenly there came a sound from Heaven . . . and there appeared to them parted tongues . . . and they were filled with the Holy Spirit.

—*Acts 2:2, 3, 4, 11*

Mary and the disciples were locked in the Upper Room praying in a spirit of expectation, and the Spirit of the Lord came in the form of fire over the heads of each one. He really sent His Love among the Apostles. The Holy Spirit is the love the Son has for the Father, and the love the Father has for the Son. The body went up to Heaven, but the Spirit became a fire. I believe the Spirit came as a fire because nothing survives a fire. No sin, no weakness, nothing. All is consumed.

At that moment, timid men became strong, fearful men became courageous, ignorant men became enlightened, and simple men became powerful. Men who lacked the courage to defend their Lord ran out into the streets and proclaimed His Name. Imperfect men, finite and frail, healed the sick, cast out demons, and raised the dead.

Holy Spirit, give me an increase of Your Gifts and the grace that assures Your Presence in my soul. Give me an awareness of the Divine Indwelling, a realization of how much the Father loves me, and transform my soul into a perfect image of Jesus.

Pray ten Hail Marys and one Glory Be.

The Assumption of Mary

Hear, O daughter, and see; turn your ear, for the King shall desire your beauty. All glorious is the king's daughter as she enters; her raiment is threaded with spun gold.

—*Psalms 44:11, 12, 14*

Our Lady is totally and absolutely united to Jesus, to the Father and to the Son. She is as close to God as any human being can possibly be. She was set apart by Her Son. Spared from Original Sin at her conception, spared the corruption of the body at her death. You can imagine her entrance into Heaven, into the love of the Holy Spirit. That's her spouse, her real spouse and she goes to be one with Him as she was always one with Him. She had reached transforming union at her conception, and with her every act of will, with every fiat uttered to God she grew closer in sanctity, in grace, and in holiness.

Imagine Our Lady seeing the Holy Spirit in infinite glory and being brought up into the very essence of God. Then she sees her Son, Body and Soul, the Word, the Eternal Word. She sees His total divinity in a new way. She fully embraces the Father. Her earthy journey ended, her merit at its peak, her beauty more ravishing than any creature ever created by God, Our Lady has reached her reward.

Mary, my Queen and Mother, I rejoice that your pure body—the Ark of the Covenant before His Birth, and a Temple of the Lord at His Resurrection—rose from death in anticipation of the General Resurrection. It is a comfort to know that you are in Heaven as my Mother with all the love and concern your dignity demands. You know the dangers of this life, you know the temptations of the Enemy, you know the weaknesses of the flesh. Help me to withstand these dangers until Jesus calls me to Himself.

Teach me, kind Mother, to keep my body pure, my mind

undefiled, and my heart detached. Let your Assumption into Heaven give me the assurance and courage to be a Christian in word and deed. Fill my mind with the knowledge of your Son's life, a compassion for His sufferings, and a zeal for His Kingdom.

Let my life be patterned after His life, and my Faith and Hope be as deep as yours. I want to stand beneath my cross exercising the same stamina with which you stood beneath His. I want my love and zeal to endure any pain and make any sacrifice. Intercede with your Son on my behalf and teach me to be like Him. Let me rise above the things of this world so my thoughts may be with you in Heaven.

Pray ten Hail Marys and one Glory Be.

The Coronation of Mary, Queen of Heaven

And a great sign appeared in Heaven: a woman clothed with the sun, and the moon under her feet, and upon her head a crown of twelve stars.

—Revelation 12:1

At the moment Our Lady was crowned Queen of Heaven, you have to wonder what happened. Did bugles blow? Did special angels suddenly arise with unimagined instruments to announce the great crowning? What pageantry there must have been. The Saints, the Angels all there to exult this woman set apart. I wonder, was Our Lady surprised?

Dear Mother, the Justice of God was not satisfied with reuniting your body and soul so you would be able to imitate

Jesus in the Kingdom. Your Divine Son, King and Lord, deigned to crown you, as Queen of Heaven and Earth. On earth you were the unknown and unheralded Mother of Jesus. Your humility astonished the Angels and confused the proud demons. It is truly just that now your greatness be manifested to all God's children.

Your one desire is to lead us to Jesus, and your one prayer is for our salvation. I am grateful for your care and sorry for my negligence. Your Coronation gives me assurance that one day I too shall be crowned with glory. God will wipe away every tear from my eyes and bestow upon me the light of glory.

Your heart was pierced with Seven Sorrows during your earthly pilgrimage. Now—twelve stars circle your head and the moon is under your feet. Obtain for me, dear Mother, the grace I need to one day enter His Kingdom and be crowned with the crown of holiness.

Pray ten Hail Marys and one Glory Be.

The

MEDITATIONS

Prayers Before Meditation

These prayers said in preparation for meditation were prayed by Mother Angelica as a young sister. They are from the PCPA Prayer Book.

ACT OF FAITH

My God, I firmly believe in Thee. I believe that Thou art truly present in the Most Holy Sacrament, and that Thy eyes penetrate the secrets of my heart.

ACT OF ADORATION

Poet profoundly imbued with this faith, I cast myself into the abyss of my nothingness, my misery, and my unworthiness, and I praise and adore Thee as my Lord and God.

ACT OF HUMILITY

Who art Thou, O my God, and who am I? Thou art the Holy of Holies, and I am but sin and nothingness. I am not worthy to raise my eyes to Thee, nor to open my lips to speak to Thee. Nevertheless, I confide in Thy boundless goodness, knowing that Thou dost not despise a humble and contrite heart. Deign, therefore, O Jesus, to give me such a heart, and I shall not become terrified because of my sinfulness, for Thou art my God and my Savior.

The Good Intention

O my Jesus, only in and for Thy Love and with the desire to please Thee and to honor Thee in the Most Blessed Sacrament do I wish to make this meditation. I acknowledge my unworthiness of the least consolation. I offer Thee, therefore, all the aridity and spiritual suffering with which it may please Thee to visit me, and ask only that Thy most holy Will may be fulfilled in me. Let me remind Thee, O dearest Jesus, that the whelps receive at least the crumbs that fall from their master's table. Therefore, dearest Jesus, do not deny me Thy Grace and Thy Love with which Thou dost sustain Thy faithful servants and brides.

Petition

Of myself, O Lord, I am not able to entertain a good thought. Deign, therefore, to illumine my understanding with Thy Light, to inflame my heart with Thy Love, so that I may banish all distractions, which I herewith renounce with my whole heart. O Holy Ghost, Spirit of Understanding, Wisdom, Counsel, Fortitude, Knowledge, Piety, and Fear of the Lord, replenish my poor heart. Holy Mary, my dearest Mother, my holy Guardian Angel, St. Joseph, holy Father Francis, holy Mothers Clare and Colette and all my holy patrons, assist me during this prayer which I unite with the divine prayer of Jesus, especially in the Garden of Olives and in the Holy Eucharist. I further unite it with the continuous prayer of Mary Immaculate and of the Angels and the saints in Heaven, as well as with that of the faithful on earth. Accept it, O Jesus, for the following intentions. . . . Eternal Father in Heaven, grant Thy most insignificant child Thy most abundant blessings. Most holy Virgin Mary, assist me, thy least and most unworthy servant.

IMMEDIATE PREPARATION

1. Invoke the Holy Ghost.
2. Humble yourself before God.
3. Recall His Presence. Begin the meditation with calmness, confidence, and humility.

TO BE A WITNESS IN THE WORLD

My Jesus, I seem to be a sign of contradiction in the world. If I follow Your commands and precepts I am considered a fool. My friends call me fanatic if I praise Your name in their presence. The standards of the world, that Your Will has placed me in, are contrary to the gentleness and humility you desire. There are times, my Lord, when my heart is heavy and my mind confused, for the way is not clear, or the path smooth.

If you belonged to the world, but because you do not belong to the world, because my choice withdrew you from the world, therefore the world hates you. . . . In the world you will have trouble but be brave: I have overcome the world.

—John 15:19; 16:33

GRATITUDE

My Lord and God, what can I do to show my gratitude for all You have done for me? Your Generosity far exceeds my desires—Your Providence surpasses my needs. Tell me, my Lord, what shall I do?

> **Give thanks to Yahweh, call his name aloud. Proclaim his deeds to the people, declare His name sublime. Sing of Yahweh, for he has done marvelous things. Let them be made known to the whole world. Cry out for joy and gladness, You dwellers in Zion, for great in the midst of you is the Holy One of Israel.**
>
> —*Isaiah 12: 4–6*

SANCTITY AND HOLINESS

What am I, Lord? I want to be holy but I am not. I don't want to fail but I do. It has been this way all my life—up and down—good and bad. Sweet Jesus, I have no reason to think it will change as time goes on. I know Your Grace and promises will always be there when I need them—always true. My dilemma is: What shall I do with Your Grace? Shall I always choose Your Will over mine?

I cannot presume on Your Mercy, for I run the risk of deadening my conscience. I can never doubt Your Forgiveness, for I would despair. Lord God, deliver me from this bondage of slavery—slavery to myself and to my ideas of holiness—slavery to my concept of perfection.

Why can't I realize once and for all that holiness is not my Gift to You but Your gift to me? It is nothing I deserve for being good for that is the duty a created being has to its Creator. It has nothing to do with merit, for one is not rewarded for the accomplishment of a duty.

O Great God, sanctity is a gift from Your gracious Goodness and since that is Your Will for me I have only to keep trying even though I fail often. Some day Your Own Holiness will lift me up above myself and I shall live forever in a state of loving obedience to Your Will and union with Your Love.

ON HUMILITY

Dear Jesus, what was it like when for the first time You felt weak and tired? When I realize Your attributes as God and consider that moment in history when You assumed my nature, it seems as if You succeeded in putting all the oceans of the world into a pint jar! It makes my poor head swim when I think of the Love it took for You to become Man! What was it like when Omnipotence felt constrained and Infinite Power had to wait?

Were You surprised when a cold shaft of wind pierced Your Body and the summer's heat made You sweat? Did You feel a twinge of rebellion when for the first time the Creator of water had to ask for a drink? Everything You created, Lord Jesus, was accomplished by a mere act of Your Will in union with the Father. How did it feel to stand near Joseph and learn how to saw wood?

To reach satisfaction in all, desire satisfaction in
nothing.

To come to possess all, desire the possession of
nothing.

To arrive at being all, desire to be nothing.

To come to the knowledge of all, desire the
knowledge of nothing.

To come to enjoy what you have not, you must go by
a way in which you enjoy not.

To come to the knowledge you have not, you must go
by a way in which you know not.

To come to the possession you have not, you must go
by a way in which you possess not.

To come to be what you are not, you must go by a
way in which you are not.

—*St. John of the Cross*

Brief Meditations by Mother Angelica

*On her nuns' feast days, Mother Angelica would handwrite short med-
itations on slips of paper and present them to each sister. These per-
sonalized messages are as profound as they are brief. Some of the nuns
saved the unique notes, which may provide a rich source of meditation
for you.*

Mary is your Mother. She guards you, protects you, and obtains many graces for you. How much do you give to her? Everything? Yes, everything. Then you have no concern. She sets your soul free.

Virtue is your yes to God. It says to all of heaven that you prefer to be like Jesus rather than like yourself. All Heaven rejoices, for you have preferred Jesus to all things.

Mary presented Jesus in the Temple and she presents you also to her Son. Every day she covers you with her mantle and presents you to the Trinity, clothed in grace.

The Angels surround you and never take their eyes away from the Father. Wonder of wonders, they are not distracted from God or from their duty to care for you. What a lesson in perfect prayer.

Never permit your soul to desire anything but God and His Glory. Self-seeking dissipates the soul and places it in a state of confusion. Seek first His Kingdom and you will find heaven within.

Rejoice in the Lord at all times because His Love is constant and faithful. We may fail Him — He never fails us. He is faithful at all times. He waits always to hear our whisper of love.

Remember the passion of Jesus when life gets hard. Think of the kind of love that would suffer so much for you.

Everything has an end. Everything passes. If you remember this, the hardest trial will be lighter.

"I have loved you with an everlasting love." If you remember this one truth then you will find the peace in your daily life.

Remember Jesus loves you. Live with Him in the Present Moment. His love is everlasting.

Pray with love—pray as you love—love as you pray. Prayer is your heartbeat in rhythm with His.

The Spirit of the Lord lives in you—breathe with His Breath that your neighbor may benefit from the fragrance of your love.

Never hamper His Work in you by questioning His Designs. Be free to fly into His arms without any barrier.

Today make an act of Love to Jesus that is the best one in your whole life: unselfish, burning, pure, holy, and without compromise. Why not? He loves you that way.

Let your joy find its fulfillment in His Work in you at every moment. Fall in love with His Will.

His Glory is shared with you at every Communion. Don't act as if you were in the pits.

Your mind is the expression of your faith, hope, and love. Let it shine bright so your neighbor can grow in His Image by the clear reflection of Jesus in your soul.

Mother's Earliest Lessons

Some of the earliest teachings and meditations of Mother Angelica are recorded in a notebook written by Sister Mary Raphael, a spiritual daughter of Mother who first met her in 1953. The following excerpts come from 1958 to 1963.

YOUR FAITH

We are praying very hard that God will increase the faith of the people who come to the chapel. We ask Him to draw them in by the pull of His Presence. Why shouldn't He do that? Didn't power go out from Him when He walked on our earth in Palestine? It's perfectly natural for Him to do that, just like it is perfectly natural for Him to work miracles. That isn't too much to ask of Him. After all, He's God, isn't He? Things like that should not surprise us. I wouldn't be surprised if a man came in here with one leg and while he was here, his missing leg grew down to meet the other. That shouldn't affect me at all. . . . Why shouldn't Our Lord do that? Who else can? "To whom shall we go?"

When Peter saw Jesus and got out of the boat to walk to Him, he wasn't conscious that he was doing anything miraculous. He was concentrating on Jesus. But as soon as he looked around and saw the storm and the waves, he went down so fast he had to cry out to Our Lord to save him. And Jesus reprimanded him for his little faith. Look through the Gospels and you'll see that all Our Lord's miracles depended on the faith of the people—not on God. Those miracles that seemed hard to perform, were so because the Lord had to lead them on until their faith was strong. (1962)

KEEPING FOCUS

No matter how much exterior work there is to do and no matter how much you accomplish in that line, you're only able to help souls in proportion to your own Union with God. There will always be more souls to help than you have time or opportunity to help. We must be careful in our striving for holiness that we do not become tainted with a seemingly pious discouragement. That is very dangerous. Because when we see more than we can do, we begin to realize it will always be so and then we begin to gaze on souls instead of Jesus—and that isn't good. (1958)

THE PRESENCE OF GOD

I don't like the expression "practicing the Presence of God." Practicing, to me, is like someone banging away at a piano each day—then they go away and leave it. No, don't "practice" being with God, just *be* with Him. It was written that when the Mother of some congregation looked at someone she didn't so much see them as see Someone in them. That's what Jesus wants of us, to be with Him, wherever we are, whatever we're doing. (1962)

TRANSFORMING UNION

In Transforming Union, Jesus takes my place and I take His Place. The Presence of God occupies the soul in this way:

1. By His Essence: a soul in mortal sin contains a Diamond (God) which is covered with tar.
2. By Grace: Sanctifying Grace in the soul makes that Diamond (God) visible.
3. By Union—Love—the rays of the Diamond (God) go out from the soul and influence others according to the degree the soul is united to God. (1962)

UNIQUE HOLINESS

Holiness, for me, is not to model myself after some Saint, but to be me, myself united to Jesus. There's nobody before or after me who will be just like me, as there are no two leaves alike on any tree—and that's from the beginning of time! That's what makes it so sad when a soul is lost. God is deprived of that particular kind of glory for all Eternity and no one else will ever fill that place. (1962)

The Temptation to Condemn or Criticize

When you are tempted to judge or condemn someone, don't argue with yourself or try to figure it out. Don't throw the incident into the committee in your head. Act like the situation happened to some third person and substitute prayers for bad thoughts, remaining in great forgetfulness of all things. . . .

When you aggravate someone today or tomorrow, your conscience will bother you. But next week it won't. Then you'll be on the road to spiritual blindness. Ten years from now, you'll be just like the people you criticize. . . . When you get critical thoughts and they begin to roll around in your mind, your conscience tells you it's the wrong thing to do. But other thoughts come to justify and excuse until you're convinced you're right. Then you're off! . . .

You can spend your whole life attached to critical thoughts. You're like a captain without a ship—and I know you're miserable. You don't fool me. You're broken-hearted inside because you don't have Our Lord. Look at Father Gerald [M. C. Fitzgerald, Retreat Master, Founder of the Servants of the Paraclete]. Ask him how to rise above these things. He does it. He's like a little child with Our Lord, watching for his crucifixion like a little kid looking for a lollipop. Father Gerald said, "The mustard seed grew into a tree that the birds of the air could build their nests in. But His branch sure has a lot of cuckoos on it." Father's Gerald's advice is: "Allow the cockle to grow with the wheat lest in uprooting you disturb also the good grain." Wait God's good time to remove the obstacles.

Forget the criticism and hold on to what lasts. St. Francis was most wise in this regard. He reached out in time and put his hands on the one thing he could hold forever—the Body of Christ. (1958)

TO JESUS THROUGH YOU

A person who is out of the Church feels very much the condition he is in, without other people treating him with an attitude of contempt or looking down on him. We must make ourselves approachable, so he can find his way back to God through us. Jesus never shunned sinners and He was criticized for it by the very people who thought they were living righteously. Pope John made himself loved in order to do good to souls. We too must make ourselves lovable. (1962)

Aridity

With your temperament, you could go way overboard with consolation. Dryness (in prayer) for you is the greatest gift God can give. He does it because He loves you. Until you realize that, you'll never be happy. (1958)

Pain

Every pain or suffering is a crossroads where the soul must choose. Either it accepts and goes forward, uniting itself to God, or it goes back on itself. Thinking of the past brings discouragement. Thinking of the future brings fear. Use your willpower and live in the Present Moment, and you'll be happy.

We must never say Jesus can't have what He wants. . . . I very often offer thanksgiving for pain, because it gives more glory to God to say thank you in times of trial and suffering than to offer it for an intention. I say several chaplets (determined number of prayers) of thanksgiving every day, but we must not only thank God for what He has done for us, but for who He is Himself. We should thank Him for His Glory and wonderful attributes, for Mary and the Angels, for the Saints and all the just — and then for me.

It is not important what happens to me — pain or joy. The only important thing is how it is giving Him glory. He must increase — but only in proportion as I decrease.

Pain is a gift, a precious jewel, direct from God. There is

no self in pain sent from God, and we must keep God in it by looking only at Him and not ourselves. I try to embrace suffering all day long, whatever form it takes. You grow stronger and stronger. When distractions come you can drive them out faster. Until you throw yourself into His crucified arms and stay there, you'll never be happy. You'll be miserable — and your misery is a grace calling you higher. (1962)

PRAYER OF ST. ANTHONY OF PADUA

O Light of the world, Infinite God, Father of eternity, Giver of Wisdom and Knowledge, and ineffable Dispenser of every spiritual grace; Who knowest all things before they are made, Who makest the darkness and the light: put forth Thy hand and touch my mouth, and make it as a sharp sword to utter eloquently Thy Words.

Make my tongue, O Lord, as a chosen arrow, to declare faithfully Thy Wonders. Put Thy Spirit, O Lord, in my heart, that I may perceive; in my soul, that I may retain; and in my conscience, that I may meditate. Do thou lovingly, holily, mercifully, clemently, and gently inspire me with Thy Grace.

Do Thou teach, guide, and strengthen the comings in and goings out of my senses and my thoughts. And let Thy Discipline instruct me even to the end, and the counsel of the Most High help me through Thine Infinite Wisdom and Mercy. Amen.

Prayers of Healing and Love

HEALING THE MEMORY

Lord Father, fill my memory with Your Compassion and Mercy. I have stored in this faculty the guilt of the past, the injuries that bring resentment and bitterness, and the remorse of unaccomplished tasks. I need to absorb Your Compassion so I may forgive those who injure me and be filled with Your Mercy.

HEALING OF UNDERSTANDING

Lord Jesus, heal my Understanding. It is so filled with doubts. I do not comprehend the mysteries of life. My understanding is often darkened by my pride and anger prevents it from reasoning clearly. I need Your Divine Light to clear away the cobwebs of ignorance that encompass my reason. I want to penetrate into the essence of every situation, see clearly the pruning of the Father, and be able to see the particular virtue needed for the moment. I become so emotionally involved at times that I cannot discern the Father's Will or see the beneficial effect of the Cross upon my soul. You have asked me to be like You, "meek and humble of heart." Will these qualities give me the light to see the right path and the faith to believe in Your Word no matter what the circumstances? Ah yes, my Jesus, if pride darkens my mind, humility enlightens it. If anger hampers my reason, meekness will give me intuition to see into the core of every situation. Let me be childlike so I can accept Your Words with Faith and simplicity. Help me to rise above the limitations of human reasoning so I may ever live in the pure air of Your Divine Wisdom. Lord Jesus, "I believe; help my unbelief."

HEALING THE WILL

Holy Spirit, heal my vacillating will. "The things I want to do I don't do and the things I don't want to do, I do." There are times I actually watch myself do something that I know is not pleasing to You. I have the light to see the better thing to do but I go right on and ignore it. It is then my conscience disturbs me and my sorrow is mixed with discouragement. I cannot honestly say I don't know the right thing to do. It is as if my soul tells me to do Your Will but my inner self tells me to do my own. Pour Your Love into my soul so I may prefer Your Desires to my own. It is love that guides the Will and if I am filled with Divine Love then our Wills can be one. Lord Spirit, I want to do all the things Jesus expects from a disciple. I want to be compassionate and merciful like the Father, meek and humble like Jesus, and full of love like You. It is my lukewarmness and self-love that make me vacillate when the time of choosing arrives. If I could love Jesus above all things, especially myself, I would find doing Your Will a loving task. I would look forward to those occasions when I would have to make a sacrifice to accomplish His Will rather than my own.

No matter how often I fail, Lord Spirit, do not tire of giving me light as to what You desire of me. With all my heart I will to do Your Will. Help me when I falter, lift me when I fall, and redirect me when I take the wrong path.

DURING DISAPPOINTMENT

My Jesus, during Your earthly sojourn when was the first time You felt disappointed? Was it over the hardhearted attitude of those in authority? Did Your human nature feel the pain that begins deep in the heart when someone You love says or does something contrary to Your ideal of him? I know You raised Your Broken Heart to the Father and gave it to Him with all Your Love. I want to give my disappointments to Him with love but I find it difficult. Sometimes, Lord Jesus, I am disappointed because the Father has not answered my prayers. When the things I ask for seem to be in my best interest I cannot understand the Father saying "No" or substituting something else for what I asked. It is then that I feel disappointed but I realize that if I loved Him as I should, this would not be so. I shall ask as a child asks its Father and be confident that whatever answer I receive is for my benefit. I shall trust His answer, for He is the only Person who loves me for myself and desires only my good. If I were the least bit humble I would rejoice in whatever answer I received for I would seek only His Will in my life and the fulfillment of that Will would be my only joy. O Jesus, do not let me spend my life thinking about what might have been. Take all disappointment out of my life by giving me the grace to see the Father's Guiding Hand in every incident and to kiss His hand with grateful love.

Lord Jesus, hold my temper in Your Hand so I may not give it to others.

Holy Spirit, help me to be faithful today or I will lose all the graces You have given me.

Lord God, I praise Your Holy Name. Let every beat of my heart be a note of love in the symphony of my life.

Lord God, though I often whisper my repentance, let me shout aloud my love.

At the End of a Trying Day

My Lord, today was a miserable day—at least in my eyes. I was impatient and irritated, not so much at my neighbor as at myself. I really don't know why except that I never come up to my expectations and it is difficult for me to admit it. But what of Your expectations? Your standards for me are so much higher and nobler than my own. Can it be that before I reach *Your* design for me I must put aside my own? Was today really one of those failures that turned into a great success? I am humbled, Lord Jesus, and down deep in my soul I know that the realization of being nothing in myself is the foundation You need to make me holy. Thank You, Jesus, it was really a good day: I came to know the real me a little better and I realized how much You are in every good thing I accomplish.

IN AWE OF GOD'S MAJESTY

My Lord, the Book of Wisdom tells me that You "have only to will and Your Power is there." What a wonderful God You are! It is difficult for my finite mind to comprehend such Power. Your Nature is so different from my own. I can produce, but You create. Everything I make must already exist in some other form before I can change it into something else but You, Great and Holy Lord, You create out of nothing! Most wonderful of all, You sustain everything You create! Whatever I make begins to age and decay from the moment it becomes what I made it to be. It certainly must be a source of wonder to the Angels when they see me proud or arrogant. It must seem like an ant telling a mountain to move over! Lord, excuse my foolishness when I step out of line. The weakness of my nature makes me think I am much greater than I am and I need Your Light to find my joy in Your Glory—the only real glory there is.

MERCIFUL LOVE

Your goodness, my Lord overwhelms me. You care for my every need and forgive all my faults. Your Love surrounds me when I fall and Your Mercy lifts me up. Though I often choose myself over You, Your Grace is ever there to prod me on to greater fidelity. When Your Mercy is extended to me, Your Love covers all my wounds and heals my soul. You make all things new, for in each succeeding moment you brush away my past and look upon my soul with infinite tenderness. You lavish gifts upon me because You are so good. Grant, my Lord, that I may be an example of Your Merciful Love.

For I, Yahweh, your God, I am holding you by the right hand. I tell you, "Do not be afraid." I will help you.

—Isaiah 41:13

UNSELFISH LOVE

My Lord, I love You and desire to love You with all my heart. What astounds me, dear Jesus, is Your love for me. Shall I ever understand it? Shall I ever realize what it means to be loved with a totally unselfish love? How can I thank You and how shall I render Your Love for love?

A PRAYER TO LOVE

My Jesus, how can I love You? If I love You emotionally, my love varies from day to day and from hot to cold. If I express my love by works, my love is petty for I cannot perform mighty deeds. The days that I decide to unite my will to Your Will and prove my love are often marked with failure and I succeed in proving not my love but my selfishness. Tell me, my Jesus, how can I bear the fruit of love in my daily life?

Whoever remains in Me, with Me in Him, bears fruit in plenty . . . as the Father has loved Me, so I have loved You. Remain in my love. If you keep my commandments you will remain in my love, just as I have kept my Father's commandments and remain in His love.

—*John 15:5, 9, 10*

LET NOT YOUR HEART BE TROUBLED

In John chapter fourteen, the Lord says, *"Do not let your hearts be troubled. Trust in God still and trust in Me."* That's an awesome sentence that you can meditate on all day. You have to do something about all your worries and frustrations. He continues: *"There are many rooms in My Father's house."* In other words, you're not aiming for the same place. You're all different. *"If it were not, I should have told you."* What a beautiful act of humility. You know, Our Lord is so, He's a *gentle* man. He saying here, "There are all kinds of rooms in My Father's house. There's a place for you, don't worry about it. There's a place for your family, don't worry about it. Trust in Me."

Why don't we think of that one sentence when we have doubts in faith, whether they're put there by our own ignorance, our own stubbornness, or whether it's the devil tempting us through a lack of faith? The Lord clearly says, "I would have told you" if it was otherwise.

And then He promises: *"I go to prepare a place for you. And after I've gone and prepared a place for you, I shall return to take you with me so that where I am, you may also be."* Do you really believe that? Do you? Oh, come on. Would you worry if you believed it? If you were going on a trip and didn't know where you were going to stay, you'd have a legitimate reason to worry. But if the Lord God, Who is all light, all truth, said, "I have a place for you" then you would be stupid to worry between this point and that final point.

Look at your worries today. You don't believe what He said. You don't believe He's prepared a place for you. You don't believe that if it weren't true He would have told you. You've got to worry; you've got to figure it out. Well, you can't figure everything out. It's stupid. Our Dear Lord stripped everything of complexities.

"If it were not so, I would have told you." That one line should clarify every doubt in your mind from now until the day you die.

One with the Lord

THE TEMPTATIONS OF JESUS

Matthew 4:1–11

There is not one facet of my life that Jesus did not experience. This includes being tempted by the evil spirit. The Lord was led into the desert for this express purpose, and to prepare himself for the combat He fasted forty days.

The pains of hunger must have been severe and it was at

a time when he was physically weak that the Tempter posed these questions. "Why not turn stones into bread? Are you not God's Son? Have you not experienced hunger? Certainly it is time to perform some wonder. No one would see you here in the desert and you have a legitimate need—yes, now is the time to use your power over creation."

"No," Christ replied calmly. "Man does not live on bread alone but on every word that comes from the mouth of God."

I wonder if Jesus was not trying to tell me that there are many ways God feeds my soul, for example: the Word coming forth from the Father. The Eternal Word (Christ) is food for my soul in the same way material food sustains my body. The revelation of God (Scripture) and the Will of God manifested in my life, moment to moment, nourishes my soul.

This is a difficult lesson for me to learn. My life is more dependent on the Word of God than on material food. I have the tendency to look upon visible reality as the only reality, and lose sight of a loving Father sustaining my very breath by His Power.

In this regard, I remember an incident in the Lord's life. He had been speaking to the Samaritan woman at the well and His disciples returned with provisions. He told them His food was to do the Will of His Father. The accomplishment of God's Will is real food for my soul because it promotes growth in Christ and sustains the supernatural life in my soul.

It is no wonder the Tempter did not understand and proceeded to tempt Christ to pride. "If you are the Son of God, cast yourself down, for it is written He will send His Angels to uphold You lest You dash your foot against a stone."

Such a manifestation of power would certainly have aroused the enthusiasm of the people and given Christ personal glory. It might have impressed those in authority to receive Him as the Messiah and start His mission of Redemption with acceptance by the majority of the people.

This course of action seems so logical, especially after waiting thirty years to begin His mission. But here again, Christ shows His complete adherence to the Father's Will, for He understood that this was not the way the Father chose for Him. The plan of Redemption called for humility and the Cross and He would follow no other path. It might not be understood but this was the only way to crush the arrogance and pride of the Tempter and to teach us how to combat our own temptations — with a calm, quiet humility. Christ answered, "It is also written 'Thou shalt not tempt the Lord thy God.'" (Deut. 6:16)

The Lord seems to be telling me something in all this. First, I must not presume on the goodness of God even though there seems to be Scriptural foundation for it. I cannot interpret Scripture to suit my own needs, especially when those needs are primarily for my own glory and pride. God is good and merciful but I cannot presume on that mercy by putting off my conversion until my old age. I must follow the Love in his time, not mine.

Second, I must use the talents and gifts given me by the Lord for the good of others with prudence and only for the glory of the Father, not my own glory or satisfaction.

Third, I must be careful of pride and a "show-off attitude"—my only concern must be to do God's Will with humility and gratitude, and to accept His Will in regard to my neighbor with loving resignation.

After tempting Christ to first misuse his power for selfish motives, and then to show off his power for personal glory, the Tempter tried the temptation that seems to succeed when all others fail—avarice, a greed for earthly things beyond the necessities of daily life. The Tempter showed him the riches of the world and said, "All these will I give You if You fall down and worship me."

Just imagine possessing all the wealth and luxury of many kingdoms for one act of adoration to the Tempter.

The Master answered quickly and firmly, "The Lord Thy God shalt thou adore and Him alone shall thou serve."

Jesus loved me so much that he permitted Himself to be tempted in those areas that I would find difficult to conquer: Selfishness. Pride. Worship of False Gods.

He gave me a beautiful example of how to act and what to do.

I must put my hope in God and look out for the good of my neighbor and not my own good. I must be humble and give the credit to the Lord for my life, talent, gifts, and possessions, and use them with prudence.

I must be detached from an excess of earthly possessions according to my state in life, love God as the only Lord and Ruler of the Universe, and seek first the Kingdom of Heaven.

The Garden of My Sin

My Jesus, I look at You in the Garden of Olives. I realize that the burden of my infidelities is upon Your shoulders and I shudder to think that I made my God grieve. I rebel when I see Judas come and give you a kiss and yet have not I proved to be a traitor when selfishness and human respect meant more to me than Your Honor and Glory. Forgive me Jesus, and grant that the suffering of Your Agony may come to my mind when temptation crosses my path so I may never offend Your Loving Heart again.

My son, have you sinned? Do not do it again, and ask forgiveness for your previous faults. Flee from sin as from a snake; if you approach it, it will bite you.
—Ecclesiastes 21:1–2

Christ's Suffering

On March 2, 1995, Mother Angelica had an asthma attack that almost took her life. She was to give the weekly lesson to her employees at the Eternal Word Television Network the following day. Instead of doing so in person, she wrote this letter to them, from her hospital bed.

Dear Family,

The Doctor has placed me on oxygen for twenty-four hours, so I am unable to be with you this morning. During the night I had a bad spell and could not breathe. It was the worst I have ever had. As I tried to gasp for some air I realized there was none. I opened my mouth in an effort to breathe. I felt I had lost the ability to breathe. My head was wet with perspiration and I cried out to Jesus: "Hold me." I stopped gasping and love surrounded me and I slowly began to breathe.

In the midst of this awesome experience and afterward I saw Jesus on the Cross—His head was tossing back and forth. His eyes and mouth were wide open. His hair was wet with blood and perspiration. His chest rose and fell as He gasped for breath. He was close to death. I realized He had allowed me to experience some of His agony. I remember thinking that His Heart broke from our sins of indifference and lack of love for Him.

For hours my body felt like a shell—empty and alone. I tell you this because it is so important that all of us love Jesus with all our heart. It is so important that we are brothers and sisters in the Lord. We must comfort Our Jesus by our spirit of love and family. Jesus loves you and so do I.

Prayers to Conclude Meditation

PRAYER OF RESOLUTION

My Lord and my God, grant that I may faithfully carry out all Thou hast effected in me during this meditation. Oh, may Thy Graces not be lost on me, but may I faithfully correspond especially to . . . which I resolve to practice most zealously. Therefore, I put this resolution within Thy Divine Heart and within the Immaculate Heart of Thy Mother Mary. (PCPA Prayer Book)

FINAL THANKSGIVING

I thank Thee, O God of my heart, for Thy manifold Graces and Benefits; for the mystery which has been the subject of my meditation. I thank Thee for having so patiently borne with me in Thy Holy Presence during this prayer. I thank Thee for the graces and the light bestowed upon me. Moreover, I thank Thee for all those graces Thou so lovingly wouldst have granted me had I been prepared to receive them and had the state of my soul and my ingratitude not prevented Thy Mercy. (PCPA Prayer book)

HEAVEN . . . CONTINUED

Heaven will be the continuation of the life we live on earth. If we are striving to live united to Jesus, death will not even interrupt the thread of this union.

ACKNOWLEDGMENTS

So many people assisted me in turning more than sixty-five years of scattered prayers into a cohesive keepsake and an appropriate reminder of the woman who inspired it, that I must thank them here.

Without Mother Mary Angelica, this work and the three that preceded it would never have been. Her ingenuity, her spiritual strength, and her deep faith are apparent on every page that I feel privileged to have edited for her. Despite the normal challenges, working on these books has been a joy. I offer them to Mother with all my love and gratitude. Mother and the Poor Clares of Perpetual Adoration at Our Lady of the Angels Monastery have been wondrous collaborators. They allowed me unrestricted access to unseen materials and permitted me to help preserve Mother's wisdom for the future. Though my love and thanks extend to the entire veiled throng, there are some that I must mention by name: Sister Maria Consolata, PCPA, who transcribed so many of these prayers and meditations (and put up with endless requests from the editor); Sister Mary Catherine, PCPA, the former Vicar of OLAM who has been a constant source of enthusiastic support and encouragement; and Sister Margaret Mary, PCPA, the succeeding Vicar of OLAM, whose devotion to Mother has been extended to me and to this work. My affection and gratitude also go out to the sisters of Our Lady of Solitude Monastery in Phoenix, the PCPA sisters in San Antonio, and my friend who started this journey with me so long ago, Sister Mary Antoinette, PCPA in Troyes, France. Their prayers have sustained my work in immeasurable ways.

On the home front, my loving wife, Rebecca, and our children, Alexander, Lorenzo, and Mariella, gave me the gift of time to assemble and edit this volume. Their enthusiasm and love sustained me throughout the long months of editing and research. (Now you know what Daddy was doing when he was locked in the office at night and on the weekends.) A big thank-you to Mom and Dad and the entire clan still toughing it out in New Orleans as well.

My gratitude runneth over for Christopher Edwards, my faithful producer and pal; for Doug Keck, my friend, executive producer, and understanding boss; for Laura Ingraham, a dear friend who never fails to make me howl with laughter on and off the air; for Joseph Looney, a lawyer with the heart of a theologian; for Arina Grossu, who helped me transcribe and arrange material with a caring eye; for my devoted webmaster, Ryan Milligan; for Mary Elkins, who keeps me talking and on schedule; and for Michael Paternostro, Jim Caviezel, Umberto and Maryellen Fedeli, and Kate O'Beirne. Your friendship and support have been an enormous consolation to me.

At EWTN, for their encouragement and aid I am grateful to my producer, James Faulkner, as well as to Lee South, Peter Gagnon, Patsy Andrews (and her crew), and to our new CEO, Michael Warsaw. I also thank the EWTN Board of Directors for their abiding support, especially Archbishop Charles Chaput and Danny Abramowicz.

I am very grateful for the hospitality of the folks at the John Paul II Cultural Center, my broadcast home in Washington, D.C. Director of the Center, Father Steven Boguslawski, OP, Deputy Director Hugh Dempsey, and Jack Heretik have made us feel very much at home. Thank you, gentlemen.

At Doubleday, my editor Trace Murphy has done it again. He has ably helmed all four Mother Angelica books with style and unfailing kindness. His assistant editor, Darya Porat, has my thanks for her labors — as do Tammy Blake, Emily Lyman, and Johanna Inwood, who did so much to publicize the book.

Then there is Loretta Barrett, my courageous agent, who first recognized the importance of bringing Mother and her message to a wider audience. She and her associates Nick Mullendore and Jennifer Didik constantly have my back. Who could ask for anything more?

Finally, my thanks to you, my loyal audience, for always being there. Stay tuned, there is much more to come . . .